Time Management Secrets the Rich Won't Tell You

Gain Freedom
Avoid Burnout
Use Time-Leverage for Wealth

(Text and Workbook)

from YourBodySoulandProsperity.com

Tom Marcoux

Executive Coach

Spoken Word Strategist

Speaker-Author of 36 books

A QuickBreakthrough Publishing Edition

Copyright © 2016 Tom Marcoux
ISBN: 0692711570
ISBN-13: 978-0692711576

All rights reserved. No part of this book may be reproduced or transmitted in any form by any means electronic or mechanical, including photocopying, recording or by any information storage and retrieval system without written permission from the publisher.

More copies are available from the publisher with the imprint QuickBreakthrough Publishing. For more information about this book contact: tomsupercoach@gmail.com

This book was developed and written with care. Names and details were modified to respect privacy.

Disclaimer: The author and publisher acknowledge that each person's situation is unique, and that readers have full responsibility to seek consultations with health, financial, spiritual and legal professionals. The author and publisher make no representations or warranties of any kind, and the author and publisher shall not be liable for any special, consequential or exemplary damages resulting, in whole or in part, from the reader's use of, or reliance upon, this material.:

Other Books by Tom Marcoux:
- What the Rich Don't Say about Getting Rich
- Discover Your Enchanted Prosperity
- Emotion-Motion Life Hacks … for More Success and Happiness
- Relax Your Way Networking
- Connect: High Trust Communication for Your Success
- Darkest Secrets of Persuasion and Seduction Masters
- Darkest Secrets of Charisma
- Darkest Secrets of Negotiation Masters
- Darkest Secrets of the Film and TV Industry Every Actor Should Know
- Darkest Secrets of Making a Pitch to the Film and Television Industry
- Darkest Secrets of Film Directing

Praise for *Time Management Secrets the Rich Won't Tell You* and Tom Marcoux:

• "Master Coach Tom Marcoux helps you make new breakthroughs to feel good, get more done, believe in yourself and enjoy each day. Create the success and prosperity you truly want!" – Dr. JoAnn Dahlkoetter, author, *Your Performing Edge* and Coach to CEOs and Olympic Gold Medalists

• "Tom Marcoux has distinguished himself as a coach, speaker and self-help author. His books combine his own philosophy and teachings, as well as those of other success experts, in a highly readable and relatable manner." – Danek S. Kaus, co-author of *Power Persuasion*

Praise for Tom Marcoux's Other Work:

• "Concerned about networking situations? Get *Relax Your Way Networking*. Success is built on high trust relationships. Master Coach Tom Marcoux reveals secrets to increase your influence."
– Greg S. Reid, Author, *Think and Grow Rich Series*

• "In Tom Marcoux's *Now You See Me*, the powerful and easy-to-use ideas can make a big difference in your business and your personal relationships." – Allen Klein, author of *You Can't Ruin My Day*

• "Marcoux's book *10 Seconds to Wealth* focuses on how each of us have divine gifts that we need to understand and use to be our best when the crucial '10 seconds' occur.... He identifies the divine gifts and shares how these gifts can help us create what we want in our lives, and the wealth we want." – Linda Finkle, author of *Finding The Fork In The Road: The Art of Maximizing the Potential of Business Partnerships*

• "In *Darkest Secrets of Persuasion and Seduction Masters: How to Protect Yourself and Turn the Power to Good*, learn useful countermeasures to protect you from being darkly manipulated."
– David Barron, co-author, *Power Persuasion*

• "In *Be Heard and Be Trusted*, Tom's advice on how to remain true to yourself and establish authentic rapport with clients is both insightful and reality based. He [shows how] to establish oneself as a credible expert."
- Arthur P. Ciaramicoli, Ed.D., Ph.D., author *The Curse of the Capable*

• "In *Reduce Clutter, Enlarge Your Life*, Marcoux will help you get rid of the physical and mental clutter occupying precious space in your life. You'll reclaim wasted energy, lower your stress, and find time for new opportunities." – Laura Stack, author of *Execution IS the Strategy*

Visit Tom's blog: www.BeHeardandBeTrusted.com

Tom Marcoux

CONTENTS*

Dedication and Acknowledgments	6
Book One: Time Management Secrets the Rich Won't Tell You	7
Wrangle Your Goals, Reserves and Relationships	33
Lift Yourself and Avoid Burnout	45
Leap Over Procrastination	55
Book Two: Use Time-Savers; Assess the Person and Still Express Compassion	63
Engage Your Positive Autopilot	67
You Don't Need Willpower; Just Use a System and Get in Motion … How You Can Get Unstuck	69
Go for the Expansion Choice and the Abundance Choice	83
Book Three: Drop Time-Wasters—Drop Hesitation	105,107
Guidance: Mark Sanborn, Laura Stack, Jeanna Gabellini, Patricia Fripp, and James Malinchak	135
Final Word, Excerpt: *Darkest Secrets of Persuasion and Seduction Masters: How to Protect Yourself...*	155,156
About the Author; Special Offer to Readers of this Book	163,155

* This table includes highlights. This book includes even more material!

DEDICATION AND ACKNOWLEDGEMENTS

This book is dedicated to the terrific book and film consultant, and author Johanna E. Mac Leod. It is also dedicated to the other team members.
Thanks to Barry Adamson II (of MyWordsForSale.com) for editing some sections. Thanks to Johanna E. MacLeod for your editing insights and for rendering the front cover and back cover. Thanks to Dave Thude for your kind friendship and insights.
Thanks for the guest authors and interviewees: Patricia Fripp, Jeanna Gabellini, James Malinchak, Mark Sanborn, and Laura Stack. Thanks to my father, Al Marcoux, for his concern and efforts for me. Thanks to my mother, Sumiyo Marcoux, a kind, generous soul. Thank you to Higher Power. Thanks to our readers, audiences, clients, my graduate/college students and my team members of Tom Marcoux Media, LLC.
The best to you.

Book One:

Time Management Secrets the Rich Won't Tell You

"He almost killed me," I said, giving a speech to some of the smartest people in Silicon Valley.

Now was the time to give them something to help them raise their game. "This guy had already hit me in the chest with his Ford F-150 truck," I continued. "He kept pushing me with his vehicle. I ended up on the hood; my feet off the street. I could see him. He was an older guy—crazy or evil or both. It was after 9 pm. Telegraph Hill neighborhood. San Francisco."

A major point of my speech to the audience at Linkedin Corporation was how to **make better decisions under pressure.** I gave the audience methods **(you'll find them in this book)** that are *more reliable* than falling back on willpower.

I'm an Executive Coach. My business is about *transformation;* my business is not about Band-Aids. So in this book, I will coach you. I'm providing something better than standard time management: *Time-Leverage for Wealth.*

Time-Leverage for Wealth includes making Life-Energizing Choices, and it's <u>not</u> just about cramming more *into your day.*

Let's look carefully at this term *Time-Leverage for Wealth.*

Time management merely involves lists and overcoming procrastination.

Instead, *Time-Leverage* is about devoting small efforts for big results. That's leverage!

Sure, many of us want to get rich. There is something better: *Wealth.*

Getting rich is *not* enough.

Wealth is what we want. Wealth is a state of being. A number of people get rich and lose it all. They didn't train for it and they didn't set up a structured daily life and a support system to Keep Their Wealth.

This book helps you create **Sustainable Wealth.**

One of my editors looked at the title of this book and asked, "*Why won't the Rich tell you their time management secrets?*" First, the topic does not come up in casual conversation.

Here's another reason: *a rich person assesses whether the person they're talking to is worth their time.* They do that automatically. Why? Because achieving significant goals requires lots of focus, effort and time.

So it's valuable to learn to **protect your time from Time-Wasters. Be sure to use Time-Savers.**

Here's the good news: *When you learn and use time management strategies,* **you'll enjoy your life more** — *you'll feel more moments of happiness and fulfillment.*

Here's a positive approach, you'll have when you use *Time-Leverage for Wealth:*

You arrive 15 minutes early at the office — before your first appointment. You have extra time so you give yourself five minutes to smile and deep breathe.

This ignites your intuition and you come up with a *Leap-Up Idea*—that is, an idea that will take your business into a whole new level of profitability.

When your client arrives, she says, "I like working with you. You're so calm and ... happy."

In my work with CEOs, I say: "I'm your Executive Coach. I'm *not* your employee. When we're in a session, I'm not your friend afraid to rock a friendship. I'm not a therapist. Some of my clients also work with a therapist. I'm in the business of *transformation*. I'm not in the business of Band-Aids. I'm here to support you to *see what you need to see* and do what you need to do to get what YOU want. That's my goal. That's my focus."

So here it is: *Time Management Secrets the Rich Won't Tell You.*

Why don't the Rich say these important details?

Here are some of the reasons:
- They don't want to appear weak
- They use strategy and keep secrets
- They do NOT know because they are like a natural athlete who does NOT analyze and communicate like a top coach
- The details do not fit the *myth* of the self-made millionaire
- They don't want to admit human failings and how they had to overcome some real internal blockages

This book is about telling the truth so you create *Sustainable Wealth.*

Here are a few of the topics covered:
Use Time-Savers:
1) Assess the Person and Still Express Compassion
2) Engage Your Positive Autopilot

3) You Don't Need Willpower; Just Use a System and Get in Motion
4) Use "Both Ends Power"—to Get Unstuck and Overcome Procrastination
5) Keep Score And Achieve More
6) Develop Your Brand to Save Time and Give a Compelling Experience
7) Drop Expectations in Favor of Agreements
8) "This is When We Get Tough"
9) Go For the Expansion Choice and the Abundance Choice

Drop Time-Wasters
1) Drop Hesitation that Arises When You Can't See Every Future Step
2) Drop Perfectionism in favor of Excellence
3) Drop Your Preconceptions and Listen
4) Drop Trying to Hold Onto Every Friend
5) Drop Fear-based "Cover all the bases"
6) Drop a Bad Mood; Replace it with the "Tai Chi Calm Down Move" or the "Tai Chi Rev Up Move"
7) Drop the Path of Burnout

These sections are designed so you can connect with the material and quickly answer related questions.

I use certain phrases so people understand them and remember the ideas. For example, as I coach CEOs, business owners and others, I express my phrase: *"Take Command, Focus Your Brand."* Even if you don't have a business, you have a personal brand (it is what you're best known for). Your clarity makes it possible to get more of what you want in life.

I'm not talking from theory. As a CEO, I lead teams in the

United Kingdom, India and the United States of America. My strategies for success are proven to work where the rubber meets the road, and that requires you to take action as you learn from my story and the *experiences** of others in these pages.

As such, I encourage you to answer the provided questions as you read along.

(* When I talk with prosperous people, we talk about *experiences*. When they ask me about my favorite times, I mention fulfilling my childhood dream of walking on the ocean floor. I had the opportunity to do that at the Grand Cayman island. I liked that better than snorkeling in the Bahamas.)

When you answer the questions I provide in this book you gain a surprising advantage: You'll learn more about yourself and how to improve your daily actions and strategies in achieving success for your life.

Let's take the next step and focus on L.I.V.E.W.E.L.L.

L – Learn your "Happy Code"
I – Intensify motion
V – Verify and say "no"
E – Expand Capacity, Productivity, Efficiency
W – Wrangle your Goals, Reserves, and Relationships
E – Energize Confidence and Delegation
L – Lift Yourself and Avoid Burnout
L – Leap over procrastination

1. Learn your "Happy Code"

Make yourself happy and surround yourself with people who are cool with that. - Larry Winget

Some years ago, I knew a guy I'll call "George." He kept telling me that he liked a quote: "I'm not happy, I'm cheerful."

The truth was: George was miserable.

Seeing something like that, my approach became **to study what it means to be happy. I realized that certain principles apply and that each one of us has individual requirements. In essence, learn your "happy code."**

First, let go of the idea that happiness equals "feeling good all the time."

People, who live authentically, feel it all: the joy, sadness, fear, courage, happy moments and more.

However, **to live a happy life, you CAN make choices and take a careful look at your beliefs.** Many of us set certain beliefs as children that do NOT serve us now as adults.

In this book, we're talking about *Time Management Secrets the Rich Won't Tell You.*

The Rich (and entrepreneurs in particular) have a certain set of beliefs that guide their daily lives. What do they believe? Some of their beliefs include:

- I can make a difference in my life.
- Failure won't kill me. I'll start again.
- Going with my intuition is best for me.
- People around me can be wrong. I will walk my own path.
- This project needs to exist, and I'm the one to lead people to make this happen.

Walt Disney walked his own path. When he first talked about Disneyland, everyone (his wife Lillian, his brother/business partner Roy O. Disney, and the board of directors) were all against Disneyland.

"But why do you want to build an amusement park? They're so dirty," his wife said.

"Mine will be clean," Walt Disney replied.

Before Walt Disney, we did *not* have Theme Parks.

Walt made a *Life-Energizing Decision* and took massive action.

Time-Leverage for Wealth includes making Life-Energizing Choices, and it's <u>not</u> just about cramming more into your day.

The Rich who enjoy a happy life make the right moves. We'll use the M.O.V.E.S. process:

M – make Life-Energizing Choices
O – organize by joy and mighty purpose
V – verify your strengths and marketplace requests
E – energize your intuition
S – shed Inappropriate Loads

1. Make Life-Energizing Choices

As an Executive Coach, I help CEOs, business owners and others accomplish Big Successes.

I learned something important: Accomplishments alone do not make one happy.

"Do your duty," my father said, some years ago.

"I do my duty, and it's not making me happy," I replied.

My father (now retired) continues to say his personal mantra, "You've got to survive."

I've responded in my mind: "I want to *thrive*."

I've learned that merely accomplishing goals does *not* make one happy. In directing feature films, writing 36 books and more, I've realized that accomplishing standard goals is *just a part* of a happy life.

So I devised a new approach to goal-setting.

The answer is to develop "Green Tranquility Goals," which are "Being Goals." [Do NOT *let yourself get stuck in only "Dark Boot Goals"—the goals, like doing taxes paperwork which just kick us in the rear. DB-Goals are merely things we must do.*]

Focus on this question: What can you do so that you enjoy more happy moments?

My clients have said:
- I devote 6 minutes a day to meditation (just sitting quietly and doing belly-breathing)
- I take a walk near trees each day
- I take a walk with my boyfriend every day
- I pray and read spiritual material
- I listen to soothing music every day

Pick specific actions that support your inner peace. So we see a *First Element of your Happy Code:* Take action for your Green Tranquility Goals—which is part of making Life-Energizing choices.

2. Organize by joy and mighty purpose

What really brings joy?

The answer became clear for me when I saw a real contrast in the following quotes:

The character Macbeth (in Shakespeare's play) says:
And all our yesterdays have lighted fools
The way to dusty death. Out, out brief candle!
Life's but a walking shadow, a poor player
That struts and frets his hour upon the stage
And then is heard no more. It is a tale
Told by an idiot, full of sound and fury
Signifying nothing.

— *Macbeth (Act 5, Scene 5*

On the other hand, George Bernard Shaw had **a different focus:**

This is the true joy in life, the being used for a purpose recognized by yourself as a mighty one; the being a force of nature instead of a feverish, selfish little clod of ailments and grievances complaining that the world will not devote itself to making you happy. ... I want to be thoroughly used up when I die, for the harder I work the more I live. I rejoice in life for its own sake. Life is no "brief candle" for me. It is a sort of splendid torch which I have got hold of for the moment, and I want to make it burn as brightly as possible before handing it on to future generations.

– George Bernard Shaw

The above contrast embodies the choice we have moment to moment. Are you making a choice *For Life?* That is, do you do that which quickens your personal energy? **Do you do that which brings joy?**

It's strange: In grammar school, I was directed to memorize Shakespeare's verses. For more than four decades I have remembered "It is a tale told by an idiot, full of sound and fury, signifying nothing."

Wait a minute! **You and I get to choose.** *We can make each day meaningful* and **signifying something great**, compassionate and loving.

We also see a **Second Element of your Happy Code:** *"This is the true joy in life, the being used for a purpose recognized by yourself as a mighty one."*

3. Verify your strengths and "marketplace requests"

Ever feel your life is like being caught on a hamster wheel? Lots of activity and no real progress.

The solution is to *focus on a powerful question.*

Some years ago, I felt overwhelmed. I turned to my sweetheart.

"I feel like a racehorse with all that I'm doing," I said.

"Run in better races," she replied.

This led to a question: What would be a better race for me? In other words ... *What would be a better fit for my skills, my preferences and what the marketplace wants?*

Soon, I thought of another question:

What do I do that's easy for me, hard for others and people want to pay for?

Now we have a **Third Element of your Happy Code:** "Ask the right questions and take appropriate action."

4. Energize your intuition

High productivity is not about merely cramming more into your busy day. It's about making Great Decisions.

How do you do that? You gain access to higher quality ideas and choices.

What counts is that you get access to your intuition.

Steve Jobs insisted that his engineers revise the iPod so that users could get to their music in just three clicks.

The idea of "just three clicks" is an example of what I call a **Leap-Up-Idea.**

The key to huge productivity is getting access to *Leap-Up-Ideas.*

You need time to think, recover and get access to your intuition.

How do you get access to your intuition? First you quiet down fear.

You can do that through daily practices of quiet time, prayer, meditation, walking near trees—whatever works for you. Additionally, **schedule in breaks.**

I say, *Take breaks or be broken.* Intuition can be silent when we allow frantic activity to fill all of our days.

Your breaks do not have to be long; they do need to be daily.

5. Shed Inappropriate Loads

"You can help a thousand, but you can't carry three on your back." – Jim Rohn

I've learned that facing reality is helpful. "Carrying three people on your back" will drain both energy and happiness from your life.

Still, we can serve family members. We CAN be kind to people. But **there is a big difference in whether we carry the person on our back all day long.**

Here's an example. *It helps to learn to shed (when possible) the inappropriate load of worry.* I arrived at the hospital and discovered that my mother was going to have her lumpectomy operation under local anesthetic. Then, I learned that her lifemate, my father, was ***not*** going into the operating room with her.

I was scared. Just weeks before, I had gone into an emergency room with my then-sweetheart. When an intern made a mistake, putting a line into my sweetheart's arm, blood went spurting out. I became lightheaded. Evidently, seeing a loved one in pain caused a physiological effect in my body.

So now, I was worried. I didn't know if I'd throw up in my facemask in the operating room.

Still, I went into the operating room and I held my mother's hand. She squeezed so hard, and I knew what to say, "Doctor, she needs more local anesthetic."

"Is she in pain?"

"Yes. More local anesthetic, please."

With more local anesthetic, my mother relaxed a bit.

My point in sharing this story is: Worry was not going to help. I needed to do what was necessary: Go into that operating room and support my mother.

After the operation, *I purposely directed my thoughts away from worrying* whether the doctor took all of the diseased cells out. We would *monitor her health* with more tests. In effect, I dropped the Inappropriate Load of unhelpful worry. [I use this thought: *Until I have the data, I will act as if it is Good News.*]

I'm grateful that my mother has been well for over ten years since that time.

Worry about pleasing everyone is an *Inappropriate* **Load.**

"You can't please everyone, and you can't make everyone like you." – Katie Couric

Drop that load! Stop trying to please everyone.

The Rich know that some friends will drift away. The fact that you're really living your life—on purpose and enjoying prosperity—irritates certain individuals. Let them drift away. You'll save your time.

I had a particular friend "George." Over more than two decades, I devoted much time to listening to George talk about his problems. I did a lot of listening because that's how I defined myself in friendship: Tom is the good listener.

One day (after other bumpy times), George said at the close of a long phone call, "That was largely useless."

"I do *not* do useless things. George, I care about you. If you have an emergency, call me. I care. Still, I will not be calling you," I replied.

Now, years later, I realize that I've saved so much time! And I recovered so much personal energy!

It's no coincidence that my life expanded after that decision.

Special Note: The Rich assess their relationships and new people they meet. Will this person enhance my life and help me reach my goals? *If not, how can I limit my time with that person?*

Director John McTiernan said that actor Sean Connery "did not suffer fools gladly." This is in line with how rich and powerful people do NOT allow others to waste their time.

The Fifth Element of your Happy Code is: Shed Inappropriate Loads.

Principle: Happiness arises from serving people and making Life-Energizing Choices.

Write answers to these 7 Questions related to your Happy Code:
1. What is a Life-Energizing Choice you can make today?
2. What can you drop from your schedule?
3. How might you enjoy helping another person?
4. What do you do that's easy for you, hard for others and people want to pay for?
5. What can be a *Green Tranquility Goal* for you—meditation, tai chi, listening to music, walking in nature, something else?
6. Are there people whom you'd do better to avoid?
7. When will you slow down for a bit and access your intuition for *Leap-Up-Ideas*?

_____

_____

_____

The L.I.V.E.W.E.L.L. Strategy
Part 2

Intensify Motion

My client Amanda created a *huge success!* She finished her first book and had it published. Her book was selling on Amazon.com. Then she had some surprising and tough feelings. Unfortunately, Amanda fell into a valley of indecision and procrastination. Now, she was stuck, and she said, "I'm not sure if I'm on the right path."

We talked for a significant time. Then I shared with her an important distinction. I drew two lines to form a vertical road on the left portion of a sheet of paper. Then I drew a matching vertical road on the right side of the page.

I said, "On the left you want a road that has the words 'certainty' and 'clarity'. The road on the right side includes 'Motion' and 'Discovery.'"

Here's an important distinction: **Motion Brings Clarity.** You take some small action. You move up the mountain, and then you can see 3 New Peaks (choices).

I emphasized, "You want to have clarity. To know for certain how everything will turn out. Still, the adventure is on the road of motion and discovery."

Here's a vital question: **How can YOU get into motion?**

Soon, I shared distinctions about these three powerful principles with Amanda:
- Motion Brings Clarity
- Intuition is friendlier when we're in motion.

- Use the Power of the AND-Universe

1. Motion Brings Clarity

Taking a small action brings you up a metaphorical mountain. You can see a different view because you're at a point where you've never been before.

From this new vantage point, you can see 3 New Peaks (choices).

I guide my clients to take a **3-Pronged Approach.** Why? Because some things you do fail to yield results you want. If you're only doing one form of marketing (for example), you can get majorly discouraged if that form of marketing fails.

On the other hand, with three marketing actions, two may be working. Also the 3-Pronged Approach prevents you from scattering your energy and attention. Scattering creates less impact.

The 3-Pronged Approach intensifies impact.

2. Intuition is friendlier when we're in motion.

When I say *intuition is friendlier,* I mean that intuition "visits" more often. You get more ideas jumping into your consciousness.

What starts intuition? A powerful question.

In my article "Learn the Secret for More Success and Happiness" I posted on Linkedin, I shared some insights about questions and answers:

"As I addressed the audience at LinkedIn, I smiled, hearing a valuable question: "What do you do if your mind goes blank?"

As a professional speaker and member of the National Speakers Association for over 15 years, I shared *Three Recovery Methods if Your Mind Goes Blank:*

1) **Have a drink of water.** (Your mind moves at 700 words

a minute and is looking for your place in the material.)

2) **Memorize phrases so you can pause in a poised manner**. (I've used phrases like: "I'll need to pause for a moment, my brain needs more RAM." ... My audience at IBM thought it was funny!)

3) **Return to the topic of your speech**, and begin with the words: "At this point, I want to emphasize ..."

I've learned that a Question opens the door to new thoughts and new methods to improve our lives.

After my speech, an audience member came up and said, "I like your idea about having a system, which can be more effective than trying to rely on willpower. I'm wanting to help my kids to learn how to focus on doing homework. What should I be thinking about with giving them more rewards?"

In response, I noted the research that points out that when you give external rewards too much, kids look on an activity that held intrinsic value for them to be "just work."

I said, "Avoid saying something like 'I'll give your $10 if you do ten drawings.' It becomes 'just work.'"

The idea is to ask your child questions like: "What do you like about drawing? What feels good about that?"

This helps the child understand that the activity has intrinsic value.

If you want to encourage someone to do a tough activity, you can ask the person: "How will you reward yourself for getting that task done?"

You can see the Power of Questions."

As I mentioned: **Intuition is friendlier when we're in motion.**

Ask yourself some empowering questions and take small actions.

Here are examples:
- What can I do to get access to more ideas?

(*Possible answer:* Write down five ideas in the morning. Write down five more ideas whenever they occur to me through the day.)
- What can I do to feel more energized?

(*Possible answers:* Take a nap in the break room during lunch. Take a walk during lunchtime. Record the *Tonight Show* and watch the episode at 8 pm on the following day.)

3. Use the Power of the AND-Universe

Amanda felt stuck and she said, "I'm just waiting to get certain about what I should put on my new business card. It's hard. I have to limit myself to one title."

"Who said, just one? It's more important to stay in the flow. In motion," I replied. "This is an AND-Universe."

So if you're beginning your business, we remember: *Motion brings clarity.* Get in front of people who can buy what you offer and have *two* titles on your business card.

Discover which of the titles *you* feel better saying to people.

For example, when I first started in my speaking and writing career, I called myself America's Communication Coach. Years later, after giving speeches to many audiences and working with clients, I learned that my better titles were Executive Coach and the Spoken Word Strategist.

I discovered this by doing the actual work with real clients.

The Rich get things done. That means the Rich are in motion.

I've guided clients to stop waiting for inspiration.

Inspiration usually comes during work, rather than before it.
– Madeleine L'Engle

The Rich know that ....
You need to get in the arena where failure and rejection are possible.

Only by getting in front of potential clients or potential investors can you learn what really works for you. So get in motion.

About Staying In Motion:
Sometimes one's life fills up. Perhaps, you need to move and your elderly parents need care, too.

I mention to my clients: "When life is so full, we can turn to *Leap-Up-Ideas*. That is, when you do not have the time to do the regular-duties toward your Big Destiny, you can still plant some seeds during the week."

By *Leap-Up-Ideas* I mean you identify something that can make your career leap forward instead of a small movement up one stair on the stairway to success.

Leap-Up Ideas **can include:**
- Who can give me an endorsement to maximize my credibility?
- Who is a hub of influence (someone who has a wide network of contacts) and how can I be helpful to that person?
- What product (perhaps, a book, video or audio) can I make to show the world that I'm skillful in the area in which I want to concentrate my efforts?

When you're in a funk, go on "Red Alert." That means you take things seriously and immediately find something that energizes you. You might find a suitable Leap-Up Idea.

Principle: Motion brings clarity.

How can you get into motion?

_____

_____

_____

The L.I.V.E.W.E.L.L. Strategy
Part 3

Verify and Say "No"

The Rich have team members *verify* if something is going as planned. The whole point is to protect one's time from being wasted by unvoiced mishaps.

For example, salespeople often arrive for a meeting and find out that the person has left for "an emergency appointment."

One of my mentors said, "Call the assistant of a prospective customer and say, 'I'm just calling to say that I'm going to be on time for my 2 pm appointment with Janet Sombodio.'" If the person failed to set the appointment then you'll find out and save yourself from a wasted trip in the car.

If you want to live an authentic, meaningful life, you need to master the art of disappointing and upsetting others, hurting feelings, and living with the reality that some people just won't like you. It may not be easy, but it's essential if you want your life to reflect your deepest desires, values, and needs.

– Cheryl Richardson

The Rich excel with people skills. By this I mean they verify who is trustworthy, and they separate themselves from false friends and people actively sabotaging their efforts.

Oprah Winfrey said, "Surround yourself with only people who are going to lift you higher."

To get rich and stay rich, you need to protect yourself from insincere opportunists.

About Saying No:

If it's not an absolute YES, it's a NO. – Cheryl Richardson

The difference between successful people and really successful people is that really successful people say no to almost everything.
– Warren Buffett

The Rich do NOT allow their time to be used up by others at those people's whim.

One of my clients was invited to attend a friend's wedding. She went AND left relatively early. Why? She's an introvert and being in a group of people uses a lot of her energy. So she protected herself and her next day by leaving early and getting enough sleep.

I am a master at setting boundaries that protect my time, energy, creativity, and emotional well-being. – Cheryl Richardson

To stay rich, you need to be strong, and you need to be at your best in High Impact Moments. You need to be able to make good decisions. Saying no to that which drains your energy is crucial.

Here's an example of how you can say no: "Thanks for thinking of me. I know your organization does great work. My plate is full. I'll have to say no. If you like, I can help you brainstorm about someone who might be match for this opportunity."

Principle: Carefully choose your words, rehearse and say 'no' effectively.

Write down the words that will help you say no effectively.

The L.I.V.E.W.E.L.L. Strategy
Part 4

Expand Capacity, Productivity, Efficiency

If you want to be rich, you cannot be normal. – Noah St. John

How do you need to be extraordinary? In these areas: Capacity, Productivity and Efficiency (CPE).

Increase your personal energy through better sleep, nutrition, exercise, recreation, loving times with friends or family, and quiet time (perhaps, meditation or prayer).

About Expanding Capacity

How do you strengthen a muscle?—You push it beyond what is comfortable. Each week, I do some weight training. No lifting and no pushups would result in the disuse and weakening of my muscles.

I was talking with one of my mentors and he pointed out *"You expand your capacity, but sometimes you need to back off from 100% to, maybe 75%."*

Why? Because you need that **25% buffer zone.** Every day things come up that surprise us that even shock us and pull our energy away. Years ago, I arrived in San Francisco to support my mother who was having surgery (a lumpectomy I mentioned earlier). I was shocked to learn that she was going to have surgery under local anesthetic and that her lifemate, my father, would *not* go into the operating room with her.

I chose to support her, and I'm so glad that I had enough sleep, exercise and good nutrition to face the situation. I did not know if I'd throw up in my facemask because weeks before I had become lightheaded when I saw my then-girlfriend have difficulty in the emergency room. When an intern made a mistake trying to put in an IV unit, my girlfriend's blood spurted out of her arm.

Still, I proved strong enough. I held my mother's hand as the surgeon cut into her chest. Her grip like a vise cued me to have the doctor to give her more local anesthetic. She relaxed a bit. I was glad that I was there for my mother.

A Different Approach to Productivity

The speaker, a multi-millionaire, turned his eyes directly on me. He held my business card and prepared to give me something valuable. The rest of the 500-person audience waited. He looked at the card then said, "Tom, I see a lot of activity on this card. I don't know how productive it is."

I took a deep breath. I noticed that my right leg was shaking, fluttering as fast as a hummingbird's wings. (Oh, the fluttering leg of my timid, nine year old self had returned.)

I would not be daunted. I resolved to apply the wisdom this speaker had imparted to me—and the rest of the audience.

Decision-making is easy if your values are clear.
– Roy O. Disney (brother and partner of Walt Disney)

When you want to be more productive, you need to know yourself better. What do you really want?

The speaker had invited me to streamline my card and my business activities.

In addition to knowing what you want, consider this

question: **What price are you willing to pay for it?**

What price will you NOT pay for something? For example, I will *not* ignore my relationship with my sweetheart. Not only will we have fun times, but we will also work with our couple's coach to ensure the good health of our relationship.

One way to know who you really are is to consciously develop your carefully chosen personal brand. Your personal brand is the answer to "What are you best known for?" It is the promise of performance. What can people count on you to accomplish that benefits them?

Here is a personal branding formula I use with various clients:

Tom Marcoux's Branding Formula:
I help people   _____
to achieve   _____
They feel   _____
My clients say   _____

Here's another way to view this:
I help people __(verb)__
to achieve __(results)__
They feel __(successful, relieved, happy about, more effective)__

My clients say: Joe is so trustworthy and smart about marketing that my sales went up 37%. [an example]

Example:
I help people create High Trust Relationships
to achieve more success and even happiness.
They feel excited and even relieved.
My clients say: "Tom coached me to get more done in 10 days than other coaches in 2 years."

Again, I want to emphasize *a great Personal Brand helps improve your productivity*. No wasted efforts here!

About Efficiency:

The first rule of any technology used in a business is that automation applied to an efficient operation will magnify the efficiency. The second is that automation applied to an inefficient operation will magnify the inefficiency. – Bill Gates

Set Criteria for Excellence

To do something efficiently, you need to know what's most important. I've come up with these questions so you can *Set Criteria for Excellence*. This is the replacement for perfectionism.

- What does a good solution look like?
- What needs to be included?
- What can be dropped?
- What do the stakeholders think is Most Important?
- What do YOU think is the Most Important?

Principle: To be more productive, *set criteria for excellence.*

Write down your *Criteria for Excellence* **here.**

The L.I.V.E.W.E.L.L. Strategy
Part 5

Wrangle Your Goals, Reserves and Relationships

"I feel burned out," said yet another business person who came up to me after I gave a speech at a company.

What's going on here?

The Rich who are both smart and happy know something: If they don't take great care, it's easy for them to burn out. **What's the solution? Juggle well your Goals, Reserves and Relationships.**

For the rich entrepreneur, it's easy to become consumed by the "shiny goals." These are the goals that pull us forward, and I call them "Golden Pull Goals."

Here's something important: **You need "Green Tranquility Goals."** By this I mean, you need goals that will nurture your being. You need to keep yourself healthy mentally, physically—and yes—spiritually.

An essential part of nurturing yourself is to take action **to have Reserves of personal energy, resilience and inner peace.**

It sounds like a tall order. It can be. Here's one thing for sure: If you don't focus on developing your Reserves, you will NOT have any!

If money is your hope for independence, you will never have it. The only real security that a man can have in this world is a reserve of knowledge, experience and ability." – Henry Ford

Build a superreserve in every area: have more than enough.
– Thomas Leonard

So that's the essence of it: Have *more than enough* (Reserves) in crucial areas of sleep, nutrition, exercise and quiet time (perhaps, meditation or prayer).

How do you have Reserves? You set goals in these areas. Additionally, you need to log your progress. For example, I log my sleep. If I'm carried by momentum and I get less than adequate sleep, I change my later schedule to get more sleep.

Where do you need to develop your Reserves?

About Relationships:

I am a shining star, and I surround myself with people who encourage my brightness. – Cheryl Richardson

The truth is your relationships are where you go to give and not just to get. Still, it's important to face the truth. Some people are too distracted, too broken or even one of the few evil people—who cannot have a healthy relationship with you. Pay close attention. Review the situation—perhaps, with a counselor or therapist you trust.

Get out of unhealthy relationships.

If you have a twisted relative, spend as little time with that person as possible. Remember, you must keep yourself strong AND then you can do good things for others.

Better keep yourself clean and bright; you are the window through which you must see the world. – George Bernard Shaw

You must push yourself to stay compassionate.

In her book, *No One Understands You And What to Do About It*, author Heidi Grant Halvorson wrote: "The researchers found [that] ... powerful people will pay attention to you when doing so facilitates *their* goal." Halvorson continued, "There is a really important insight in this research. For the powerful, your *instrumentality* is key. Frankly, it is all that matters. What can you do to help powerful people reach *their* goals? ... If they invest time and mental energy into really 'getting' you, what is the potential return on their investment? ... Instrumentality isn't about being nice—it's about being useful."

Here's a time management secret that the Rich don't talk about: It is creating and nurturing important relationships that really facilitates success.

Here's the insight I'm bringing to you: **You must push yourself to stay compassionate.** Why? If you lose touch with your humanity, you'll "blow up." You'll treat other people harshly by reflex.

Further, if you lose your compassion, you'll even lose compassion for yourself. You'll create your own misery. Lots of money and no happiness—that's an awful plan.

How do you keep your compassion alive?

It's been proven that if you shift your focus, you CAN see things from another person's point of view. How? Use these words to activate the shift: **"How would I feel if I ____?"**

For example, some adults were having difficulty with their elderly parents who bitterly complained during every visit.

One woman said, "I thought about how would I feel if I was stuck in a bed 17 hours a day and felt pain most of the time." She reported that *her perspective shifted.*

Another way to keep your compassion alive is: Take

good care of yourself. If you're in pain, if you're exhausted, you do *not* have the space to pay attention to another person nor his or her situation.

If you find that you're having trouble being compassionate towards others, connect with a part of yourself that needs healing.

Negotiate to Agreements

Good relationships have good patterns of negotiation. The truth is each individual has had a unique experience of a life journey. Sometimes, it's amazing that we understand another person at all. Why? Every word we speak is tinted by our own personal experience.

I say "purple" and people have different immediate reactions:

- Purple? *Purple Rain*—that's a movie that Prince starred in.
- Purple? That's a girl's color. Men don't wear that.
- Purple? Oh, it's so pretty.

Here's a big drain on relationships: Holding expectations. For example, recently I had a conversation with my sweetheart. I mentioned how I was upset that a relative was lying about a situation and pretending that I had failed to do something appropriate.

"That's not how he sees it," she said.

Now, I could hold an expectation that she, by reflex, backs me up. But she had a different point of view.

So I said, "I'd prefer that you'd back me up on this. But your thoughts are your thoughts. Your perceptions are your perceptions."

That was my short cut of saying that "I won't hold an expectation that you see the world in exactly my way."

Anyway, she responded: "I don't agree with what that relative did." (See? She does back me up.)

I choose to leave it at that.

Here's a powerful secret: Drop Expectations in Favor of Creating Agreements.

If I feel, and hold the expectation, that "it's only fair" that my sweetheart does some of the paperwork this might cause trouble.

Instead, I can ask, "Will you agree to doing the first sorting of these receipts?"

If she does not agree, then I can drop the expectation.

Often, she avoids agreeing to something she feels she cannot guarantee. That's understandable.

We can keep up our dialogue until we do come to an Agreement.

Do not manage people, manage agreements. – Steve Chandler

About Asking for a Favor
Rich people are adept at asking for favors and returning favors.

One of my mentors taught me three things to include: a) ask gently for the favor, b) do NOT remind the person of what you did for them before, and c) leave the person with a way to "get out of it."

People do NOT like to be backed into a corner. They rebel against anything that feels like force or being compelled. Be sure to say something like: "Would you give me an introduction—perhaps, by email to—Sam Stephland? I know you're busy so this might not line up."

Principle: Take action to balance out your Goals, Reserves and Relationships.

What do you need to change to improve your Reserves and Relationships?

_____

_____

_____

_____

_____

The L.I.V.E.W.E.L.L. Strategy
Part 6

Energize Confidence and Delegation

Confidence to some is a Holy Grail. "Oh, if I just had more confidence, I could be successful," an audience member said during a partner-work session during one of my workshops.

Just tonight during my workshop, one person said, "Self-esteem is confidence."

During the next minutes, I said, "Confidence is something different. Self-esteem is the experience of feeling *worthy* of the blessings, and self-esteem is the experience of feeling *capable* of improving your life."

If you don't feel worthy of good things happening in your life, you are unlikely to take action and to stretch.

If you don't feel capable, you won't take action. No action equals no improvement.

In reviewing this I note that *confidence is related to feeling capable.*

But here's a vital point: **Confidence is NOT comfort.**

It's valuable to learn, rehearse and develop the ability to adapt to situations as they arise.

Still, *when you feel that you CAN adapt, you may develop some confidence.* However, you can still feel a bit nervous or concerned. You can still feel uncomfortable.

Self-esteem is the disposition to experience oneself as being

*competent to cope with the basic challenges of life and of being worthy of happiness. It is confidence in the efficacy of our mind, in our ability to think. By extension, it is confidence in our ability to learn, make appropriate choices and decisions, and respond effectively to change. It is also the experience that success, achievement, fulfillment—happiness—are right and natural for us.
– Nathaniel Branden*

So real confidence arises by setting small tasks for ourselves and accomplishing them. This is evidence for yourself that you ARE competent to cope with the basic challenges of life.

Confidence arises from doing actions and ADAPTING. Again, confidence is NOT comfort. **With enough experiences of adapting, you're able to trust yourself to be able to adapt to new situations and challenges.**

I realized early on that if I wasn't out of my comfort zone, I wasn't thinking big enough. - Tory Burch

I think of confidence arising from C.A.N.: "Call on help, Adapt, Nurture yourself." The Rich know that the right coaching can make an empowering difference.

Confidence arises when you get in motion. (In another section, I share the principle I coined: *Motion Brings Clarity*.)

About Delegation:
The Rich get more things done. That does *not* mean that they do all the vital things themselves. **The Rich are adept at delegating effectively.**

Nothing is impossible for the [person] who doesn't have to do it himself. – A. H. Weiler

We'll use the N.O.W. process of effective delegating:

N – nurture the person to good performance
O – organize natural check-in points and agreements
W – wrangle benefits for the person taking action

1. Nurture the person to good performance
Delegating goes wrong when we fail to devote enough attention, time and effort to it. You need to make sure that the person to whom you delegate CAN do the work well. You also need make sure that person gets something from it. For example, I make sure that my illustrators will complete great work that will shine in their portfolios. I mention, "Our team members watch your back and check you work so you'll be proud to have this image in your portfolio."

2. Organize natural check-in points and agreements
"Is that a realistic deadline?" I ask before I close the conversation about a deadline with one of my team members. We set up realistic deadlines so the person can succeed. I also make sure that the person says, "I agree. I can and I will be able to get the work done by 10 pm Wednesday, April 17th." **Agreements are better than a manager holding expectations.** An agreement must be created that is both realistic and has the team member's commitment. To put this in few words, people rebel against expectations. That's the reason that creating an agreement *with* a team member is vital.

Additionally, organize a schedule of natural check-in points. I say, "I want you to feel good about this work. I don't want you to lose time in going down a blind alley. So when is it a good time for us to check-in with your work-in-progress?" You'll notice how I truly involve my team member in the process so he or she can succeed!

3. Wrangle benefits for the person taking action

If you say, "Their benefit is their paycheck!" and you do not think of the rest of the picture, you'll miss chances to delegate effectively.

Researchers note that people quit jobs based often on the lack of feedback, appreciation and recognition.

As my team completed the graphic novel *Crystal Pegasus* (available on Amazon.com), I posted completed pages on a private blog so all team members could see each person's progress. I had four colorists who each could see the level of quality achieved by the other colorists. One benefit was that all team members could be proud of the work completed.

I've noticed that no one became motivated by hearing: "Join us, we're doing something mediocre!"

Here are some benefits you can provide:
- Praise for good work
- Recognition for good work (team members' names on the front cover of *Crystal Pegasus*)
- a promotion
- a bonus
- copies of the finished product
- special perks (I gave out T-shirts of the *TimePulse* logo to team members working on that science fiction project)
- special knowledge and coaching
- personalized help for the person's career (I've helped people gain jobs [interview well] at Donna Karen in New York and Telltale, the video game company that created the *Game of Thrones* video game.)

Delegating is both art and science. Study how to delegate effectively and you'll save time and have a highly productive team.

Principle: To delegate well, pay close attention that you nurture your team member so he or she can be successful with the task.

How can you make sure that your team member has all he or she needs to succeed? How can you take care to provide praise, recognition, appreciation, special benefits for work that is well-done?

_____

_____

_____

The L.I.V.E.W.E.L.L. Strategy
Part 7

Lift Yourself and Avoid Burnout

The Rich do *not* allow negative people to extinguish their flame and enthusiasm for their project or business.
Here's one of my favorite quotes:
30% will love you.
30% will hate you
30% couldn't care less.
– Gabrielle Reece

As an Executive Coach, I frequently emphasize the above quote. If my client acknowledges that 60% of the people won't be with her, anyway—**she now has freedom**. I call this using your "30-30-30 Shield." This "Shield" guards your self-esteem. You realize that your work is often judged by a person whose perception is clouded by their own internal issues. Your work can have merit *beyond* what that person can perceive.

If you always do what interests you, at least one person is pleased. – Katharine Hepburn

Merriam-webster.com notes that *burnout* is "exhaustion of physical or emotional strength or motivation usually as a result of prolonged stress or frustration."
Exhaustion often arises because we're not doing enough

to build our own emotional reserves.

Are you doing the same thing day after day because of the fear that you're going to lose your current position or current audience? This road can lead to burnout.

See if you can add something new and creative to your life.

I don't begrudge any artist for getting an audience. I'm sorry, I never found that poverty meant purity. – David Bowie

The late David Bowie went through periods in which he was severely criticized by his own fans and critics. Why? He changed! He tried new things.

Lift yourself by <u>not</u> denying the reality of disappointment; instead, you condition yourself to work with it and continue to rise.
The question is: How?

I developed something I call **"Celebrate Someone Disagrees" Celebration.** You can do something nice for yourself. Have a cup of coffee at your favorite coffeehouse. Visit with a friend.

Proclaim that you're celebrating your courage, that you put something out into the world.

We say "someone disagrees" because we realize, as noted in the quote from Gabrielle Reese, that at least 60% of the people will not like your work anyway. If you don't courageously finish projects and put them into the world, no one will be able to disagree with it.

Let's celebrate your creativity and courage.
Today, I encouraged a client by saying: "There's an old phrase: 'Some people go to the ocean with a teaspoon; some bring a bucket.' Sharon, you've got a big destiny. You're

going to help people trade-in that teaspoon for something bigger."

I invite you to take in the idea that **you have a big destiny, too.**

We avoid burnout by remaining curious, making stuff and showing it to people.

I first discussed this in an article at my blog YourBodySoulandProsperity.com

Achievers Rising: Avoid Burnout and Rise to New Heights of Success

"What surprised you about coaching people to big, transformational successes, Tom?" my friend Carl asked.

"Some of my clients, in the past, would hit a valley after a big success," I replied.

In recent years, I work with clients to help them be strong and avoid burnout. In fact, I use this phrase: "This is when We Get Tough."

First, we face reality. We acknowledge these Myths that arise out of what people imagine success to be:

Myths:
1) You'll feel like you have arrived.
2) You'll have no more problems.
3) No one misunderstands you.
4) You'll feel good all the time.
5) You'll stay excited all the time.
6) You'll never have any doubts that you're on the right path.
7) You'll never wonder why you feel disheartened, disorientated or disappointed (the 3 Ds).

When I speak on the topic "Achievers Rising: Avoid Burnout and Rise to New Heights of Success," I share the A.I.M. process.

A – arrange and rotate challenge, activity, recovery
I – intensify self-nurturing
M – move

1. Arrange and rotate challenge, activity, recovery

The idea is that you can get tired, but you do not let yourself get exhausted. Exhausted can be in body or spirit or both. The solution is to be deliberate about your Recovery Actions. I log my sleep, exercise daily and eat salad for breakfast (willpower is stronger earlier in the day).

Now it's your turn: What do you do to ensure you have enough Recovery in your life?

Some people fall apart when they first achieve millionaire status—including Jim Rohn and Tony Robbins. They lose big sums of money and have to endure a real struggle on their way back to the top. Additionally, bestselling author and entrepreneur Randy Gage talked about how his life fell apart during some successful times.

What is the solution? Maintain structure in your daily life and rotate Challenge, Activity and Recovery.

Challenge can bring new energy into your life. One of my clients became excited about a new writing project. Some coaches might say, "Shut that down. That's a distraction."

Instead, I said, "We'll use that excitement. It will spread so you have the energy to do what you must do." We also make sure that the new project "does NOT take over."

I'm an OptiRealist. I know that optimism can provide the fuel for achievement. Still, I'm a realist. I help my clients see the whole picture and see the end game. Then we build the strategies to make positive things happen.

Energy is still crucial. I have a phrase: **What you dread gets you ahead.** In line with this principle, we realize that one needs energy to do the tough things in life.

It's the rotating of challenge, activity and recovery that helps my clients continue to soar and reach higher and higher levels of success.

Remember, Challenge, Activity, Recovery.

You might say: "No C.A.R.; no go."

2. Intensify self-nurturing

When I work with CEOs and business owners, I see them easily gravitate to the "shiny goals." These are goals that are fun to talk about. I call them *Golden Pull Goals.* In order for you to avoid burnout, you need another form of goal—what I call *Green Tranquility Goals.* These are "Being Goals." On a daily basis, you do something that strengthens you. My clients use activities like quiet time, meditation, painting, journaling, praying, walking near trees, watching something funny on video (enjoying laughter everyday), yoga, tai chi, and other nurturing actions.

For my clients who are introverts, I help them put some quiet time into their daily lives. They must recharge while they are alone—away from other people. For an introvert, being with other people is expensive in terms of personal energy.

Additionally, I guide my clients to avoid the "After a Success, a fall into a valley." The solution is to overlap one's goals. Here's an example. Before I finished my 35th book, I started writing my first YA novel. I did not fall into a post-project spot of emptiness.

Now it's your turn. Find out what nurtures your feelings of fulfillment. When do you feel creative and on track? How can you "overlap your goals"?

3. Move

"Don't worry about it. I'm just procrastinating a bit and trying to find clarity," my client Sarah said.

"I hear you," I replied. We talked for a bit more. Then, I shared this: "**Motion brings clarity.** Try things. Get in the arena. See how things feel."

I added, "You get to the top of a peak and then you can see three new peaks (new choices). You couldn't see the choices when you were not in motion and you were at the bottom of the mountain."

The most successful people I've interviewed get into the arena where they can face rejection and failure—much more than other people.

After I give certain speeches, some business owners come up to me and say, "I just need to find the right salesperson." A bit later in the conversation, I mention: "How can you train a salesperson if you don't know what works? People like to join successful ventures. You need to get involved in sales and marketing. You need to develop the pitch (and a *good dialogue*) and watch people's faces. Founders of companies do well when they learn to sell what they're offering. They learn to use compelling stories."

When I say "move"—I mean Get in Motion. Learn, rehearse, practice, get coaching, get in front of potential customers/clients.

A powerful part of "Move" is to Shift Your Perception

For example, we avoid burnout when we drop certain expectations. Success is NOT static. We do not simply "arrive."

I've learned that Connecting to the Present Moment is crucial.

It's helpful to realize that this is an AND-Universe. [I wrote a book entitled *The Hidden Power of the AND-Universe*.]

Here are brief comments about Shifting Your Perception:

1) You can be Grateful AND feel uncomfortable.

For example, as I write these words, I'm grateful to be connecting with you. AND, I'm in pain. I recently broke a tooth (on a soft cookie—oh, the irony).

Still, I avoid wallowing in the pain. I shift my thoughts to so much in my life that I'm grateful for now.

You can also be grateful for what is absent. I have a couple of friends who tried to talk me out of writing a lot of books. They drifted away. What a relief! An old phrase holds: Some people brighten a room by leaving it.

2) Experience the Shift in Perspective that Opens the World to You

Imagine the possibilities when you shift away from fear to intuition. First, let's look at the differences:

Fear says, "Contract, hide, don't take any risks."

Intuition says, "Expand, experiment, take an appropriate risk."

Life becomes an adventure when we're NOT shackled by fear.

If you do something that scares you, it is often coming from a place that might create a button [an impact on the audience].
– Leonard Nimoy

The universe often rewards us for the scary choices.
– Pharrell Williams

3) Discover the Power of Enjoying the Moments as they come and go.

Your task is not to seek for love, but merely to seek and find all the barriers within yourself that you have built against it. – Rumi

I've learned that removing the barriers to being fully alive in this present moment is the vital difference that helps an achiever keep on achieving—and to avoid burnout.

My successful clients (and those whom I interview) also discover the value in helping others and turning their focus away from their own personal concerns. Burnout often arises when we get caught up in personal frustrations. Years ago, I knew someone who would go into a rage when he had "a bad workout." He said, "My day is ruined." At that time, I remembered an old phrase: "You're upset because your canvas is too small."

Instead, we can expand the canvas of our life when we're engaged with demonstrating kindness to others. For example, in my book, *What the Rich Don't Say about Getting Rich*, I interview Michael Hsieh (president of a venture capital fund) who shares his delight in supporting children with few resources to have access to an extraordinary education (at a chartered school).

Be sure to include a focus on something beyond yourself.

Remember to use the A.I.M. process:

A – arrange and rotate challenge, activity, recovery

I – intensify self-nurturing

M – move

Earlier, I mentioned, Success is not static.

Pay close attention to how your life is going.

Rotate challenge, activity and recovery so that you'll continue to soar and reach higher and higher levels of success.

* * * * * *

Avoiding Burnout and Use 3 Particular Secrets of the Rich

Here are three particular **Time Management Secrets of the Rich:**

#1 – Assess other people

#2 – Assess yourself

#3 – Learn to play the game AND *to unplug to avoid being consumed.*

The Rich *assess whether a new person is a) an asset to help the rich one reach their goals or b) a 'brittle' person (and one does well to limit one's exposure).* To put it in few words, the "brittle" person may have personal biases and resentments about prosperity. Such a person may create upsetting situations because they attempt to feel "superior to money-grubbing rich people." **The rich person moves on from such people.**

A number of rich entrepreneurs have had to learn a lot to gain funding and run businesses. So *they have had to assess their weak areas* and learn to improve personal behaviors. Or they've learned to get team members to take care of certain areas of a business.

Secret #3 – Learn to play the game AND to unplug to avoid being consumed directly relates to avoiding burnout.

The solution for burnout is to consciously increase one's self-nurturing through appropriate rest, refreshing activities and quiet time away from business activities. In another area of this book, I talk about nurturing relationships. Healthy relationships can often provide a respite from overwork.

In remembering "Motion brings clarity," what new actions can you experiment with—so you move forward in a positive direction?

_____

_____

_____

The L.I.V.E.W.E.L.L. Strategy
Part 8

Leap Over Procrastination

"Procrastination is the foundation of all disasters." – Pandora Poikilos

Procrastination habits are like mud. They hold us back. You might say that procrastination is like a distorted mirror. Upon reflection, we could conclude: "That's not me. Or at least that's not the best version of me."

Instead, we can "leap over" those habits. When I say "leap over procrastination," I mean that we're going to jump away from those habits that create procrastination in our day.

So if you're procrastinating, ask yourself:

Is it that I –
- Don't know how?
- Don't feel like it?
- Don't want to do it?
- Am afraid to do it?

The answers will guide you to take a small action forward. Here are examples:
- Don't know how? (Google it! Get a coach.)
- Don't feel like it? (Take a small step. Put on energizing music. Promise someone you love that you'll do it.)
- Don't want to do it? (Break it down into something tiny to do. Need to write an article?—write a sentence. Don't

let yourself get stuck. If I don't have the right word, I write "__MORE__" and I keep on writing a first draft.)
- Am afraid to do it? (Get support! Line up your friends. Rehearse the first minute of a speech with one friend. Practice a story from the middle of the speech with another friend. Hire a coach. Take a class.)

"Keep your hand moving." - Natalie Goldberg (on writing)
One time I was working with a client, "Sam." He had fallen into a rut. He told me a story about how his childhood "made him this way."

I followed my intuition and said, "Time to stop telling me that story. That story hurts you, Sam. It keeps you stuck. Instead, **tell me a new story.** A story that empowers you."

"I just keep my hand moving," Sam said, echoing the Natalie Goldberg's comment I related above.

"Yes! That's a new story. A good story!" I said.

Technique #1: Procrastination Solution — Set A Pattern
At one point, I decided to write my first YA novel, *Jenalee Storm*. I set a pattern: Write 300 words a day before I allow myself to sleep. It worked: I wrote 17,561 words in 51 days.

Technique #2: Don't let it get on the To-Do List
On numerous occasions, I've received a book from a colleague to write a review. The moment it arrives in the mail, I immediately study the book and write a draft of a review article. I exclaim: "No hesitation!"

I want to avoid *The Pain* of having a review article "hanging over my head."

Now it's your turn. What would you want to *Never Make It* to your To-Do List?

Technique #3: Identify Your Procrastination-Pattern and "Get Around It"

At one point, I found that I would return from an evening walk with my sweetheart and a family member would have the TV on. The easiest thing in the world was to sit down and watch TV.

So I had to get around this. I'd grab a cup and run up the stairs saying "Time for me to teach my online class."

Upstairs, I run water into the cup, and I'd sit down and immediately get to work on the computer. I'd take sips of water every so often.

Technique #4: Employ a One Page Business Plan to energize your actions

Would you like to get more done and feel better about your life? When you focus on what you really want and develop a focused-plan, you'll feel better because you'll have both marching orders and true clarity.

On the other hand, without a focus point, we scatter our energy. I've developed the **One Page Business Plan** that I carry with me every day.

The ultimate benefits of a One Page Business Plan are:
- more productivity
- time savings
- clarity
- focus on activities that generate personal good feelings and fulfillment
- focus on activities that generate profit

An old phrase is: "You get what you think about most." When you use a One Page Business Plan, you're thinking in a focused and positive manner.

Here are the topics that go on one 8.5 x 11 inch sheet of paper (suitable for a wallet or purse):

One Page Business Plan

- Mission:

- Top Goals with Due Dates:

- Ultimate Goals:

- Current Areas to Feel Good About and Feel Excited About (What works)

- Current Leadership-Growth Areas (includes keeping team members strong and happy)

- Current Areas to Measure

- Current Areas to Improve

- Current Areas to Watch Carefully (monitor and improve)

- [Your First Name,] What Are You Looking Forward to Experiencing and to Feeling?

- 3 Levels of Goals: Good, Excellent, Amazing!

- Effort Goals . . . Result Goals

- Other Notes:

© Tom Marcoux   Tom's Blog: BeHeardandBeTrusted.com

The *One Page Business Plan* is the center of *Focus-Point-Mastery*. The idea is to approach your daily life like you're a master of *Time-Leverage for Wealth*. It's really about you becoming skillful in making things happen that increase your joy and fulfillment.

Since there are 11 elements of the One Page Business Plan and I want to summarize the overall process, I'll now provide a few details per section.

1. Mission

It's best when your mission is beyond just making money. For example, my company's mission is: *We create energizing, encouraging edutainment for our good and humankind's rise.*

I include "our good" because strong and happy people make things turn out better for customers. Further, I make sure that team members fulfill some personal goals. It keeps them motivated to devote their best efforts.

2. Top Goals with Due Dates

Due dates are crucial; otherwise, things are too vague. Without due dates, productivity suffers.

3. Ultimate Goals

One of my ultimate goals is for my fantasy-thriller franchise *Jack AngelSword* to be so successful so that near the end of my lifespan Disney will want to buy my company. This would insure that millions of people would be served by my work beyond my lifetime. How fun!

4. Current Areas to Feel Good About and Feel Excited About (What works)

Never underestimate the power of good, empowering feelings to carry you forward through any tough times.

5. **Current Leadership-Growth Areas (includes keeping team members strong and happy)**

Every leader has weak areas and blind spots. It's good to identify details to work on. Good leaders develop loyal and productive teams.

6. **Current Areas to Measure**

I emphasize: *"Don't guess. Measure for success."* For example, I identified a target of writing 400 words a day which alerted me that I had 170 days to go on a certain project. A benefit of measuring your progress is that you raise your own morale!

7. **Current Areas to Improve**

People who are serious about increasing their joy and fulfillment monitor how they're currently doing. They also identify how they can get better at what they do.

8. **Current Areas to Watch Carefully (monitor and improve)**

In business, leaders are advised to pay attention to Key Performance Indicators and "critical measures." Two such measures can include number of sales meetings and closed sales. Which critical areas do you need to monitor and improve?

9. **[Your First Name,] What Are You Looking Forward to Experiencing and to Feeling?**

Imagine this: you can clearly see what all of your big efforts are going to bring to your life. Such clarity can motivate you on a daily basis. What do you really want? Research data shows that many people simply want to feel happy and secure. How will accomplishing your business goals bring you such feelings?

10. Three Levels of Goals: Good, Excellent, Amazing!

Some people set goals that are too extreme. Others set goals that are too low and un-motivating.

I've learned that it's better to set three levels for goals: Good, Excellent, Amazing!

Here's an example:

One author I know sells 25 books each month. She can set a "Excellent" goal of 300 books. Then, for "Amazing!" she can set 4,000 books sold per month. To reach for the 4,000 level, her thinking must expand. Now, she's thinking of ideas like: "How can I team up with other authors so that we can promote our respective books to each other's e-lists?"

Three levels of goals gives you the space to think bigger and allow the universe to give you "happy surprises."

11. Effort Goals . . . Result Goals

In sales, an Effort Goal can be "make 30 marketing calls this week." A related Result Goal might be "gain three new clients." We notice: You can't get a Result Goal without taking action on an Effort Goal.

You can be proud of yourself for your actions on Effort Goals regardless of whether you meet a Result Goal this week or next month. The truth is: Result Goals are often based on things out of our control. The good news is that we can control our personal efforts toward Effort Goals.

* * *

Here is the essence of the One Page Business Plan:
We are motivated by what we want to feel.

We generally change ourselves for one of two reasons: inspiration or desperation. – Jim Rohn

Another way to look at this is:
What do you want to feel?
And what do you want to STOP feeling?

Many people are wired in such a way that they'll do more to end some form of pain than make the efforts for something vaguely positive.

The One Page Business Plan helps you identify your clear, focused plan of action.

I've noticed that many people will put more effort into planning a vacation than planning their life.

But this is NOT for you.

Use a One Page Business Plan that's focused on business-related goals, and you're likely to expand your success. More success may lead to more vacations!

Principle
Using a One Page Business Plan helps you focus on critical factors to improve both your business efforts AND your feelings of fulfillment.

Power Question
What would you put into the categories of your One Page Business Plan?

Write down your first ideas about your business goals that you can achieve AND actions that provide you with feelings of fulfillment.

Book Two: Use Time-Savers

Use Time-Savers #1

Assess the Person and Still Express Compassion

The rich and successful people I've interviewed have demonstrated incredible focus.

Plus they're careful about their time.

This leads to a **Double-Approach: Assess the Person and Still Express Compassion.**

About Assessing a Person:
Lots of people want to ride with you in the limo, but what you want is someone who will take the bus with you when the limo breaks down. – Oprah Winfrey

Surround yourself with only people who are going to lift you higher. — Oprah Winfrey

The Rich learn—often through hard experience—that certain individuals "talk a good game," but they really have no room in their heart for you.

The Rich test people and watch to see how the person reacts. For example, celebrated actor Frank Langella wrote about an experience he had as a young man. Frank acted quickly and saved the life of the son of a rich man. After the son was safely in the hospital, the rich man pulled out his checkbook. He asked Frank how much money he wanted.

Frank refused. (By the way, the rich man was testing Frank and was finding out if Frank had a price.)

The rich man said, "You will not leave this room without my giving you something."

Frank grabbed a cheap still camera: "How about this?"

For years afterward, the rich man treated Frank as part of the family.

What is the central question to help you assess whether another person is helpful or trouble for you?

Use the question: **Does this strengthen me?**

Marina, a client, told me that every time she sees her mother she leaves feeling worse than before her visit. Ultimately, Marina realized that her mother simply is *not* capable of acting in a loving, kind manner. Marina learned to seek guidance and comfort from her Aunt Sophia. The solution is to spend less time with her mother.

[** **Note:** The question *Does this strengthen me?* applies to other choices.
- Watching many hours of television. Does this strengthen me? No.
- Studying books in my field. Does this strengthen me? Yes!]

The Rich do NOT allow people to waste their time nor their energy!

About the Second Part of the *"Double-Approach: Assess the Person and Still Express Compassion*:

Let's say you assess that a person is too needy and is an "energy-vampire." **You can still express compassion.** Be fully present with the person for the five or ten minutes you're with him or her. Listen closely. Be respectful and kind. Then graciously excuse yourself and leave that person's presence. What a relief!

After your brief encounter, remind yourself to avoid letting that person get on your calendar.

[*It's also true that some people are so emotionally twisted or "brittle" that you do better to graciously get out of their presence fast.* One time I was at a meeting and someone came up to me and expressed a bunch of things he thought that I do wrong. I listened for a bit. Then I said, "I've heard you. I'll ponder this. I was trying to be helpful. I see that we're not a match. I must step away. I wish you well." I quickly walked away from that person. I later learned that this person was treating a number of people in a shabby way. I'm glad that I was strong enough to avoid reacting and sending negativity back. I avoid "practicing anger."]

Let's Talk about a Real Love Relationship

It's true that in a real love relationship sometimes a partner goes through a rough patch. During that time, the person may be different—more prone to anger or depression-related behaviors. This person may be hard to endure. Perhaps, the person is grieving or going through a mid-life crisis. Still, there is real love present in the relationship.

To love someone is to see a miracle invisible to others.
– Francois Mauriac

I invite you to observe carefully and find something to praise in your loved one. (Or simply listen.) For example, everyday I praise my sweetheart for something, and I thank her for something she does (or did), too. These are like deposits into our emotional bank account.

Principle: Assess the person and still express compassion.

How are you using your time? Are you wasting your time on "brittle-people"? Can you reduce time with people who drain your personal energy?

_____

_____

_____

_____

Use Time-Savers #2

Engage Your Positive Autopilot

What do you do automatically? I remember some years ago when I'd go running with my father. After a run, we would go into a convenience store, and my reward would be orange cupcakes. Wait a minute! A good run might let go of 200 calories but the orange cupcakes packed in 400 calories. Trouble! I learned to replace oranges cupcakes with oranges (the fruit).

We'll use the P.O.P. process:

P – Proclaim
O – Organize a Positive Trigger
P – Power-up Your Behavior Sequence (a replacement)

1. Proclaim
"I eat salad for breakfast," I've shared with numerous audiences.

In the morning when I open the refrigerator door, my own words echo in my mind, "I eat salad for breakfast."

So I automatically reach for spinach and small tomatoes to toss into a bowl.

Be careful with whom you proclaim your automatic, empowering behavior. Still, reducing your intention to a few words—and speaking those words aloud—empowers you.

2. Organize a Positive Trigger

Researchers note that human beings are tossed around by triggers all day long. If I see potato chips on the dinning room table, that can be a problem. It's better to keep those things in a cupboard!

Instead, **set up a Positive Trigger**. In the morning, opening the refrigerator door is my Positive Trigger. I think: "I eat salad for breakfast." Then, as I mentioned, I automatically toss spinach and tomatoes into a bowl.

3. Power-up Your Behavior Sequence (a replacement)

I've heard a number of people lament, "I've got to break this bad habit."

Here's something more powerful: "I am *Replacing* the bad habit."

For example, at one point, I'd fill one glass with 15% soda and another glass with 100% water. I'd drink both beverages. In this way, I was **replacing the habit** of just drinking soda.

When you set a Behavior Sequence, you avoid having to make the same decision again and again. This is what it means to engage your Positive Autopilot.

Principle: Carefully choose your Positive Trigger and make the decision *one* time. (This is engaging your Positive Autopilot.)

What can be a Positive Trigger for you? How can you construct your positive Behavior Sequence?

Use Time-Savers #3

You Don't Need Willpower; Just Use a System and Get in Motion

"I just need more willpower. Then I'll write my book everyday," my client, Anna, said. In a discussion, I introduced Anna to the *Power of Having a System.* Research at Stanford University and elsewhere demonstrates that as the day goes on willpower "wears out." Dr. Kelly McGonigal writes that willpower is like a muscle that suffers from fatigue as the day goes on. I take advantage of this and eat salad for breakfast. And that is my "System"!

Myth: It's okay to wait for "One Focus," passion and motivation.

A Way You Can Get Hurt:

You lose the precious minutes of your life. You fail to get vital experience as your explore possibilities.

Get Real Principle: Get in motion; set a system; and set a game. (You don't need willpower when you have a system.)

Get in motion; set a system; and set a game. I use a mnemonic device to remember this: "MSG" as in *motion, system, game.* [Yes, MSG also stands for a food additive. Still, *Motion, System, Game* is an additive that BUILDS your life.]

1. Motion

Some people view the individuals like Steve Jobs, Tony Robbins, Martha Stewart and others to be a "force of nature." You do *not* need to be a force of nature. *To make progress, we just need you to take one step after another.*

3. System

Your system can take into account when you have energy. One of my clients writes her next book during her lunch hour. She found out that she feels too tired to write upon returning home in the evening—after her regular job.

Author Steve Chandler reports that he got a client to get invoices done by simply setting a pattern. The client now sends out an invoice immediately after a client call. The client does not stop even for the restroom until the email with the invoice is sent. Willpower is *not* required.

2. Game

A number of people allow their lives to fall into a pattern in which they cannot win. It helps to make a strategic plan so you can "Make it a game you can win." Pick a goal that is a stretch. Still, observe reality. Pay attention to feedback.

We need to make a game out of earning money. Without it, we are bound and shackled and our choices become limited.
– Bob Proctor.

How can you get in motion? How can you "make it a game you can win"? What kind of system can you set up?

Use Time-Savers #4

Use "Both Ends Power" — To Get Unstuck and Overcome Procrastination

Does the idea of setting a quota and having to fulfill it bother you?

The idea is to use *a Quota AND a Daily Journal of Victories and Blessings.* Why? If you only focus on a quota sometimes you'll go to bed feeling bad because you missed hitting your quota. For example, if your quota is to make 10 marketing phone calls, but you only hit 8, then you might feel bad.

However, if you write down 8 phone calls completed in your *Daily Journal of Victories and Blessings,* you can celebrate what you DID accomplish. Write down the good parts of your day in just 1.5 minutes — just before you go to sleep.

I refer to Quota plus a Daily Journal of Victories and Blessings as "Both Ends Power." Picture a ruler with quota on the left side. Your Daily Journal is on the right side of the ruler. I picked a ruler because you are measuring your incremental progress. Your Daily Journal helps you pay attention to your positive action. In this way, for 1.5 minutes a day you are celebrating your Daily Progress.

This ties in with using your brain effectively. Research shows that it takes 10 seconds of focused attention on something positive so that detail goes into your long-term memory.

So you are solidifying your impression of your progress — in your own mind. This is vital!

More About Getting Unstuck and Overcoming Procrastination

I also introduce my clients and audiences to *Top Six Targets.* *These* are your most vital tasks. I often say, "2 for you, 2 for family, 2 for work." If you complete these six tasks, you have a Good Day!

WARNING: Keep your To-Do List away from Your *Daily Journal of Victories and Blessings* **and Your** *Top Six Targets.*

Why? If you view your To-Do List just before you go to sleep, you'll feel sad. When I was in college my To-Do List was a To-Don't List and a Guilt List.

I'm talking about Getting Unstuck and Overcoming Procrastination. So I invite you to take 2 minutes every night and write up your *Top Six Targets* for your next day. It works! It keeps your top priorities front and center. [For more about this, see my book *Emotion-Motion Life Hacks.*]

And for 2 minutes every night, you write in your *Daily Journal of Victories and Blessings.* A victory is something you accomplish. A blessing is a gift like a surprise phone call with a friend. **These 2 minutes ensure that you go to sleep happy.**

Principle: Write your *Top Six Targets* in 2 minutes just before sleep, so you have your top priorities/tasks identified and ready to go for your next morning.

How will you make a *Daily Journal of Victories and Blessings* into a welcome part of your day? Are you attracted to certain designs? [Some people like flowers. Others like a design related to a theme park or a favorite film.]

Use Time-Savers #5

Keep Score and Achieve More

"How did you write 36 books, Tom?" my friend Carla asked. I use three methods that I refer to as my K.I.T.

K - Keep Score and Achieve More
I – Itemize a Progress Log
T – Think "Top Six Targets"

The Rich are masters of focusing on the most important. The following three methods help you accomplish such laser-focus.

1. Keep Score and Achieve More
People wouldn't go bowling if they couldn't see the pins drop.
– Zig Ziglar

During a speech I attended, Zig emphasized that we need to take care to accomplish certain daily tasks. His comment about bowling relates to much that we do in life. We need to see that we're making progress—which will help us keep going through the rough patches.

I keep score of many things: steps walked each day, sit-ups and pushups completed, words written and more.

2. Itemize a Progress Log
What gets rewarded, get repeated. – John E. Jones

Here's an example: As of this moment I've written 32,322 words of this book. Yes, I know! I log the number of words I write per project everyday.

I write everyday. My Progress Log for another writing project reads 17,061 words. I'll write at least 300 more words before I close my eyes and sleep tonight.

A Progress Log, according to researchers, actually provides endorphins for many people. They simply feel good upon seeing their progress. In a sense, that's a form of reward.

We can do even better by planning on giving ourselves a reward as we hit a series of milestones.

3. Think "Top Six Targets"

In college, I went to bed sad every night. Why? My To-Do List would not get shorter. It was a To-Don't List. It was a Guilt List.

After college, I came up with a solution: *Top Six Targets*. For 1 ½ minutes before I sleep, I write down Six most important tasks.

With audiences, I say: "2 for you, 2 for family and 2 for work." If you accomplish these six vital tasks, you'll have a good day.

Principle: To be more productive, focus on the most important with a *Progress Log* and *Top Six Targets*.

What are the Most Important tasks for your next day?

Use Time-Savers #6

Develop Your Brand to Save Time and Give a Compelling Experience

Build something 100 people love, not something 1 million people kind of like. – Brian Chesky (Airbnb billionaire)

When you start a company, it's more an art than a science because it's totally unknown. Instead of solving high-profile problems, try to solve something that's deeply personal to you. Ideally, if you're an ordinary person and you've just solved your problem, you might have solved the problem for millions of people.
– Brian Chesky

What is your brand?
You might think about a product or service that you offer. You also have a Personal Brand. I wrote a book on developing your personal brand titled: *Secrets of Awesome Dinner Guests: What Walt Disney, Steve Jobs, Oprah Winfrey, Albert Einstein, Martin Luther King, Jr., Helen Keller, and John Lasseter Can Teach You About Success and Fulfillment. (The Power of Your Personal Brand).*

Here I'll share details about *Create a Compelling Experience for the Person and Save Time.*

Picture this. Two people meet for the first time. Andrew asks: "So Cynthia, what do you do?"

"I help people recover money, save money and find

money so they can take that Dream Vacation or start their own company if they want to."

"How do you do that?" Andrew asks.

"As an accountant, I ask a lot of questions to help a person, perhaps, someone like you, discover ...."

You've just observed the proof of "Is it compelling enough?" When the other person asks, "How do you do that?" you know your expression of your personal brand is compelling.

Here's how you save time: You find ways to help the new person find themselves connected to what you're talking about. Cynthia includes her listener by saying, "perhaps, someone like you..." The word "you" can be used well.

Whenever you say something, people are in their own mental space. They do have subconscious questions that I call *The 3 Ws:* "Who are you? Why should I listen to you? What's in it for me?"

Be sure to develop your communication about your brand or personal brand to answer quickly those questions.

By the way, your personal brand is the answer to the question: "What are you best known for?"

Your personal brand is a promise of performance. What can people count on you to do?

Here's another example:

"What do you do, Tom?"

Tom: "I'll answer that. *And* I'm curious: What are you looking forward to?"

Sam: "What? A vacation? Work?"

Tom: "Whichever has more of your attention."

Sam: "I'm looking forward to snorkeling in the Bahamas."

Tom: "Is it your first time?"

[Tom and Sam continue talking for a bit.]

Tom: "That sounds like so much fun. Sam, to answer your

question about what I do: I help people get more experiences like snorkeling in the Bahamas."

Sam: "How do you do that?"

Tom: "I help people fulfill Big Dreams. I do that primarily as an Executive Coach and the Spoken Word Strategist ...."

My point here is that it works well when you get the other person talking, and they get excited about what means a lot to him or her.

Principle: Develop your communication to create a compelling experience for the listener. Get them to ask, "How do you do that?"

How can you connect with what's important to your listener? How can you seize his or her attention?

_____

_____

_____

Use Time-Savers #7

Drop Expectations in Favor of Agreements

"I'm so disappointed," my friend Susan said.

"What happened?" I asked.

"Joe forgot again. He didn't remember to get the dry cleaning on his way home. What does he think—that I'm his slave?"

When I hear comments like this, I'm reminded that it's truly easy to hold expectations about what we want our loved ones to do. We expect them to be thoughtful. We expect them to take extra care. We expect them to remember what is important to us.

Do we expect them not to be human? Do we expect them not to be individuals who have experienced the world in different ways?

My point is: *Expectations can get us into trouble.*

What is the solution? **Substitute agreements for expectations.**

Creating agreements works wonders. Up-vibe your personal and professional relationships by learning to create agreements instead of expecting others to do things (and then being disappointed when they don't). – Steve Chandler

How does this work?

You actually ask the person, "Do we have an agreement?"

For example, I work with contractors and interns to do illustrations for my graphic novels. I have a conversation with them about a deadline. "So what is realistic for you—10 pm on Thursday, April 19th?" I ask.

Further in the conversation, I ask, "Is Friday at 10 pm more realistic?

"Yeah. That should work," the illustrator replies.

"Sounds good. So Friday April 20th at 10 pm you'll have the new version of the *Jack AngelSword* swordfight image done. Do we have an agreement?"

"Uh ... maybe I should say, Saturday at 4 pm. I do have a friend staying over on Friday night ..."

When you ask for the person's agreement, he or she takes the situation more seriously. You are NOT imposing an expectation from the outside.

If something goes wrong, you blame the agreement. You say something like: "Oh, it looks like the agreement did not work. So let's see how we can make the next agreement work."

Sidenote: With my contractors, I say, "If you get it done early, you're a hero!"

The Rich know how to delegate well, and they avoid lost time to miscommunications.

Principle: Create agreements and avoid trying to impose expectations—from the outside.

How can you change your expectations into creating agreements?

Use Time-Savers #8

"This is When We Get Tough"

Some time ago, I was concerned. My client had become stuck. Yes, I had guided her and helped her make her big dream come true. Still, she stopped moving forward.

I thought about how I might have to really push her.

Then a new idea, a better idea, arose in my thoughts.

In our next session, I said, *"This is When We Get Tough."*

The Rich often discover that a big success does NOT feel the way they imagined it would feel. A big success does *not* eliminate all feelings of doubt.

To get tough, we implement daily actions that keep us strong.

We must all suffer from one of two pains: the pain of discipline or the pain of regret. The difference is discipline weighs ounces while regret weighs tons. – Jim Rohn

(Responding to a question about why a number of icons including Michael Jackson, Whitney Houston and Prince died relatively young...) Don't let this [music] business fool you. It looks like a delicate flower on the outside. This is a thorny bush. And to crawl up on that stage every night to do what we love to do, it's not the stage that kills us. It's getting to the stage or maintaining the pressure before you get to the stage. It's the fighting with the money side, the agents side, who's going to take the money, who's trying to get to the money, who's trying to be

next to me. Are you sincere with being around me?
– Lionel Ritchie

What are daily actions that keep us strong? Exercise, good sleep and nutrition. We also need recreation and to avoid numbing out too much with food or television.

Every day one of my clients practices certain martial arts moves to keep her flexible and strong. A good plan!

With daily disciplines, you can respond faster and do better in High Impact Moments.

For example, I rehearse every day for speeches and meetings.

Don't wish it was easier, wish you were better. Don't wish for less problems, wish for more skills. Don't wish for less challenge, wish for more wisdom. – Jim Rohn

Success is nothing more than a few simple disciplines, practiced every day. – Jim Rohn

Principle: Pick daily disciplines to keep you strong.

What daily discipline can keep you strong?

Use Time-Savers #9

Go For the Expansion Choice and the Abundance Choice

"I'll say this in a few words. Stop telling that story. That's a Death Story. We need you to replace it with a Life Story. A story where you're proud of yourself, where you feel you're making progress. That Death Story is hurting you. Stop it! You CAN move into your new chapter of life," I said.

"Wow ... let me take a couple of moments to take this in," my client Allen said.

Earlier in my coaching journey, I might have softened how I said the above material.

However, *I must be fearless* for my executive coaching clients. I tell them: "During a coaching session, I'm not your employee. I'm not your friend. A friend would be afraid of rocking your friendship. I'll help you see what you need to see. I'm not holding back. I'm in the business of *transformation;* I'm NOT in the business of Band-Aids. I'm your advocate for what YOU want in your heart. I'm *not* a psychotherapist. Some of my clients have a therapist *and* have me as their executive coach."

I then share: "*You will achieve more than you believe.* When you have someone who believes in you like I believe in you, **You WILL achieve more than you believe.** I know this to be a fact because I had three instructors in high school who saw more in me than I could see.

- One taught me psychology: I earned a degree in psychology
- One taught me English literature: I wrote 36 books, screenplays—and I directed feature films
- One taught me theology: I wrote a college level online Comparative Religion course that I've been teaching for over 14 years.

I know: You will achieve more than you believe."

My point here is that you do better when you go for the Expansion Choice and the Abundance Choice.

What can break that? Fear.

The oldest and strongest emotion of mankind is fear, and the oldest and strongest kind of fear is fear of the unknown.

– H. P. Lovecraft

Fear stifles our thinking and actions. It creates indecisiveness that results in stagnation. I have known talented people who procrastinate indefinitely rather than risk failure. Lost opportunities cause erosion of confidence, and the downward spiral begins. – Charles Stanley

Let's look at this distinction:

The voice of fear: contract, hide, take no risks

The voice of intuition: expand, experiment, take an appropriate risk.

The idea is to make space so you become aware of your voice of intuition that guides you toward the Expansion Choice.

The Expansion Choice creates *The Double Wow!*

Your Double Wow includes:

a) You say: "Wow! This is exactly why I'm on the planet"

b) The other person says: "Wow! This helps me so much!"

The Rich go for more, different and better. How do they get that? They purposely focus on Expansion Choices. A number of Expansion Choices lead to more abundance of income, healthy friendships and inner peace.

Life in abundance comes only through great love.
– Elbert Hubbard

The key to abundance is meeting limited circumstances with unlimited thoughts. – Marianne Williamson

A [person] is rich in proportion to the number of things which he can afford to let alone. – Henry David Thoreau

About "let alone," let go of trying to get people's approval. Follow your personal path.

Principle: Listen to your empowering intuition and pick the Expansion Choice.

What would *The Double Wow!* look like in your life?

_____

_____

_____

Use Time-Savers #10

Use "Better Than Zero"

It does not matter how slowly you go as long as you do not stop.
– Confucius

The Rich, in particular, entrepreneurs plan ahead. One of my mentors said, "Ideally, you would divide your attention as 50% to current cash flow and 50% to building your business (building assets)."

Here's the truth. If you devote, even just one hour toward building actual assets each week, you will move forward. My company focuses on intellectual property with our entertainment franchises *Jack AngelSword* (graphic novels) and *Jenalee Storm* (YA novels). With franchises, there is no ceiling on potential products and profits.

Constant effort and frequent mistakes are the stepping stones to genius. – Elbert Hubbard

Better Than Zero ties in with "Learn While You Explore"

Many of my best speeches arise out of things I learned by exploring and trying new things.

The first time I directed a promotional video with an Olympic Gold Medalist as the spokesperson, I was shocked.

Right in the middle of the fourth take the Olympic Gold Medalist stopped saying the words, got up, left the set and refused to continue. (I will not identify this person—it would cause trouble for friends of mine.)

I was stunned. I had never met this person before and the producer had made all the arrangements. I was a "hired gun" as the video director. *I was accustomed to working with professional actors* and performers who WANTED to do an excellent job.

I later learned that this Olympic Gold Medalist was sick of it all—the photo shoots, all of the media interviews....

I learned something important: **Don't Assume. Make sure everyone is on the same page before the event.**

Knowing what I know now, I would have had at least a five-minute sit-down meeting with the producer and Medalist. I'd ask, "How are you expecting this to go?"

If the Medalist said, "I'll give you two takes," I would reply: "Then we'll make sure they're good ones. First, I need to ask you a couple of questions before the camera starts recording ..."

Because I know that Olympic athletes put in extreme efforts, I had assumed that this particular athlete would be focused (like an actor) on doing a great job. Wrong assumption.

In working in the film/TV industry, I've also learned this:

The Rich know this Secret: "You want to get rich and Save Time? Learn to deal with people with Big Egos."

So make sure that you have that pre-event meeting so you can make sure people are on the same page.

It is literally true that you can succeed best and quickest by helping others to succeed. – Napoleon Hill

The pre-event meeting is a way that you can make sure that you help others succeed.

Still, I'm glad that I've taken action because even a small action helps you get to "better than zero."

Principle: Take a small action and achieve "better than zero."

What small tasks can you do so you create "better than zero"?

Use Time-Savers #11

Save Time: Choose "No Resistance"— and Choose to Listen

The college student came at me with a karate punch. This was a demonstration for the benefit of his fellow students. First, I did a karate block. By the way, we did this in slow-motion. I said, "We'll do this in slow-motion so I don't get hurt." The college students enjoyed laughing at that one.

"With a karate block, we have force meets force. We both get bruised," I said.

We redid the process but this time I did an Aikido maneuver: I sidestepped; the force went past me. I guided the arm and started taking the student toward the floor. I stopped the movement, and invited the students to applaud their classmate.

Aikido involves having "no resistance" to the attack. Instead, you guide the force so it's harmless to you.

We are not going to succeed in everything we attempt in life. That's a guarantee. In fact, the more we do in life, the more chance there is not to succeed in some things. But what a rich life we are having! Win or lose, we just keep winning. – Susan Jeffers

The Rich know when to "cut their losses." An old phrase holds: "Stop betting money on a losing horse."

The Rich know to avoid wasting time and money.

A big waste of time arises when we offer resistance and get into needless arguments.

If you can, with a friend, family member, or business

partner, agree to some detail. You might say, "Yes. You're right: I can be distracted. I do make that mistake. How about we have a meeting 20 minutes from now so I can give this situation and you my full attention?"

That's an Aikido move. You do not meet force with force.

Choose to Listen

You'll save a lot of time when you listen first—before mishaps and misunderstandings can occur. In my book, *Connect*, I wrote about *Listening Blockers*. I'll share some brief insights here.

Listening Blockers:
- Judging – You jump ahead and think that what the person says has no merit.
- Defending – You defend yourself and your actions. You're talking and you're not listening.
- "Me, too—One Up" – Instead of admitting that the person has a point and has found your error, you go on the attack and say, "Yeah—well, you do that all the time!"

When you notice that you've fallen into one of the above Listening Blocker traps, take a breath and then ask a gentle question:
- That sounds frustrating. What else bothered you about the situation?
- What else do you need me to know about this?
- How can I help to make this better?

Principle: Choose nonresistance and listen more.

What triggers you? How can you do more listening?

Use Time-Savers #12

Often Choose "Assertive" NOT "Aggressive"

My client Louise needed to negotiate to recover money from a company related to an unfair late charge on a bill.

Louise told me, "I dread this. I don't want to get angry and have to push the other person to help me."

"Then do *not* get angry. Imagine that the person is a good friend and you're going to brighten her day because she's going to get the chance to help you," I said—as part of an extended conversation. My point is: *You prepare yourself* to start from a *positive* and firm position.

Helping people separate "assertive" from "aggressive" can be an extended process.

Here I'll provide some brief comments about methods you can use to be assertive.

First, you need to identify what you want.

Second, find ways to be firm AND pleasant.

I'll actually praise a manager and say, "Thanks for making this process as pleasant as possible. I appreciate your help."

Look at the difference between assertive words and aggressive phrases:

- *Aggressive:* "Your company is horrible! It's criminal how you charge extreme fees! And then you have the gall to charge me a wrong fee! Damn this ..."

- *Assertive:* "That's not acceptable. How can you keep a good customer happy?"

Other assertive phrases:
- We need you to do better than that.
- Is that the best you can do?

Smart Rich People Are Assertive

One can be firm AND pleasant. You can be pleasant and straight to the point: "Here's what I'm looking for: please waive the late fee and return the interest amount to my account. I'm hoping you're empowered to do that."

Staying silent is like a slow growing cancer to the soul and a trait of a true coward. There is nothing intelligent about not standing up for yourself. You may not win every battle. However, everyone will at least know what you stood for—YOU.
– Shannon L. Alder

If you live your life to please everyone else, you will continue to feel frustrated and powerless. This is because what others want may not be good for you. – Beverly Engel

If the Rich feel powerless, they do something about it!

We can say what we need to say. We can gently, but assertively, speak our mind. We do not need to be judgmental, tactless, blaming or cruel when we speak our truths.
– Melody Beattie

Offer a "This or that solution"

People don't like to be cornered. One time a family member bought some jewelry at a "junk jewelry store." They would not provide a refund even though the jewelry discolored my family member's finger and proved to be not sterling silver.

I said, "Let's take care of this quickly. You can provide a refund or my family member can pick up some other things in the store in place of the original purchase."

The manager opted for my family member choosing other products in the store.

End of transaction. By the way, I asked my family member, "Please don't get anything else from this store. The products are junk. Okay?"

She agreed.

Principle: Know what you want, choose your words carefully, rehearse—and be assertive.

Write some effective assertive (not aggressive) words here which you can use to resolve something in your life:

_____

_____

Use Time-Savers #13

Your Springboard to Optimal Performance

I coach a sports psychologist who in turn coaches Olympic Gold Medalists. There is no Olympic athlete who avoids having a coach.

Top people in business have coaches. They know that they need to be at their best during *high impact moments*, which include closing a sale, getting new team members and successfully negotiating what you want.

Myth: Optimal Performance is possible without coaching and rehearsal.

A Way You Can Get Hurt: You can waste time, lose money and burn bridges if you go into *High Impact Moments* without coaching or rehearsal.

Get Real Principle: Get coaching and do some form of rehearsal *daily*.

Author Tony Robbins has talked about "The Science of Success and the Art of Fulfillment."

These two elements are central to much of the executive coaching I do.

"The worst days of those who enjoy what they do are better than the best days of those who don't." – Jim Rohn

What is it that you enjoy about your work? Become strategic in focusing on what only you can do. That's when you start to have a business!

Are you consistently getting coaching? Are you rehearsing for some High Impact Moment that's coming up on your calendar?

Use Time-Savers #14

Study and Rehearse to Avoid Costly Mistakes

Years ago, my parents arrived in Reno, Nevada and found that their hotel was a significant distance from the primary street in Reno. My mother was a bit frail and this was troublesome news.

I talked politely with a hotel manager. No solution was forthcoming. I said, "That's not acceptable. How can you make this better?"

Then the hotel manager found a solution that involved moving my parents to a sister-hotel. How did I know to say what I said? Through study. I had read about negotiation practices.

Spectacular achievement is always preceded by unspectacular preparation. – Robert H. Schuller

There are no secrets to success. It is the result of preparation, hard work, and learning from failure. – Colin Powell

One important key to success is self-confidence. An important key to self-confidence is preparation. – Arthur Ashe

I study and rehearse every day. Why? I have no idea what new opportunity or challenge is going to arrive the next day.

I want to be as ready as possible.

Rich people I have interviewed are curious, and they pay close attention to their surroundings.

To acquire knowledge, one must study; but to acquire wisdom, one must observe. – Marilyn vos Savant

I believe that people make their own luck by great preparation and good strategy. – Jack Canfield

Rich people want something so much that they're willing to devote themselves to developing extraordinary skills.

Study strategy over the years and achieve the spirit of the warrior. – Miyamoto Musashi

What can you study and rehearse to make you more prepared for surprising opportunities and challenges?

_____

_____

_____

_____

_____

Use Time-Savers #15

Take Action and Do NOT Wait to "Believe"

You need to put what you learn into practice and do it over and over again until it's a habit. I always say, "Seeing is not believing. Doing is believing." – Brett Hoebel

My client gave up. That is, before she met me. Twenty years before our meeting ... at 15, Felicia gave up on her dream to be a writer. Why? She had dyslexia. Then she met me and I supported her to write a paragraph ... then a two paragraph blog post ... then 52 blog posts. Soon after she had a manuscript, and a senior acquisitions editor at a major publishing house took the book manuscript to the committee.

As of this writing, my client has five published books.

Here's the vital point: She did NOT believe she could write a blog post, she did not believe she could write a book —**But she did NOT wait to believe.** She just took small steps.

You do not have to be certain before you begin.

I emphasize: *Motion Brings Clarity.*

At Stanford University, Bernard Roth (academic director of the d.school at Stanford) leads students in an initiative called "Entrepreneurial Design for Extreme Affordability." At one point, the students started with a question: "How can we keep incubators for pre-mature babies operational in truly poor areas of Nepal?"

They learned the power in **"Reframing the question."**

The real question they discovered was "How do we keep pre-mature babies warm enough to stay alive?" Most incubators in Nepal were no where near the areas where the mothers needed them.

So instead, as Bernard Roth tells it: "[They designed] a miniature sleeping bag with a removable pouch containing a block of waxlike material that, when heated, becomes a liquid that remains at the required temperature for nearly five hours. The heat could be supplied by boiling the pouch in water, which could be accomplished without electricity."

My point in sharing this story with you is to invite you to get in motion. You learn and develop solutions on your journey.

Principle: Take action. Do not wait to "Believe."

How can you take action today and stop telling the story that you need to wait to "become certain"?

Use Time-Savers #16

Learn to Negotiate Well

You don't get what you deserve, you get what you negotiate.
– Chester Karrass

"I can't say that. It would make me a b___h," my client Amanda said.

We continued in our conversation. I shared that for her to simply say, "That's not working for us. Can you do better than that?" was NOT being aggressive. *It was being assertive which is a positive thing.* My client did use these words and she was able to secure a better payout to her parents from an insurance company.

The Rich know that to increase one's income it's vital to learn to negotiate well.

I wrote a whole book on negotiating titled: *Darkest Secrets of Negotiation: How to Protect Yourself, Overcome Intimidation, Get Stronger, and Turn the Power to Good.*

Here I'll share briefly three vital components of negotiation—in the A.I.M. process:

A – alert yourself to your L.A.R. and M.S.P.
I – intensify rehearsal
M – make it a game you can win

1. Alert yourself to your L.A.R. and M.S.P.

Here are ideas first mentioned by author and master negotiator Herb Cohen: "L.A.R." and "M.S.P."

L.A.R. stands for Least Acceptable Result. If you were selling a used car and you felt that the Least Acceptable Result was $5,000, you would find anything over $5,000 to be "a win."

M.S.P. stands for Maximum Supportable Position. You are being sized up by the person on the other side of the table. If you ask for something astronomical, they might just conclude that you're crazy or at least a complete amateur, whom they want to avoid.

Do your research. Identify a good L.A.R. and a good M.S.P. Then you'll start from strength.

2. Intensify rehearsal

Spectacular achievement is always preceded by unspectacular preparation. – Robert H. Schuller

Before you go into a negotiation, prepare what you're going to say. With my clients, we prepare what I call *"If-Then Patterns."*

Here's an example:

If the other person says, "This costs too much."

Then I say, "Compared to what? Compared to a product that breaks in six months or compared to how my product will last more than seven years—saving you money each year. Let's go over the numbers."

I rehearse every day, usually for speeches. I also rehearse before a big meeting with a potential client who will pay me thousands of dollars up front.

Often, I have a driver so I rehearse in the car on the way to one of my speeches or meetings.

What situations could you improve by your rehearsing prior to the event?

3. Make it a game you can win

At one point, one of my clients found that a medical organization was going to overcharge her. I guided her to call the organization back at different times. The goal? To get a different manager on the phone. The *third* manager quickly resolved the issue. My client could not "win" with the other managers.

So many people give up. They do not use strategy to make a negotiation turn out in their favor.

But this is *not* for you.

Observe the situation carefully. Talk with someone empowered to "keep you a happy customer" if you're in such a situation.

Principle: Prepare and rehearse for negotiations.

What details of an upcoming negotiation do you need to prepare? With whom can you rehearse?

_____

_____

_____

Book Three: Drop Time-Wasters

Drop Time-Wasters #1

Drop the Desire for Everyone to Like You

There is a lie that acts like a virus within the mind of humanity. And that lie is, 'There's not enough good to go around. There's lack and there's limitation and there's just not enough.'

The truth is that there's more than enough good to go around. There is more than enough creative ideas. There is more than enough power. There is more than enough love. There's more than enough joy. All of this begins to come through a mind that is aware of its own infinite nature.

There is enough for everyone. If you believe it, if you can see it, if you act from it, it will show up for you. That's the truth.
– Michael Beckwith

I shared the above quote because I've observed that people who live from the above-noted premise get significant resistance from others.

To put this in few words, *rich people often face resentment from others who have not found how to get more productivity out of themselves.*

As a number of authors note: It's easier to dislike someone who acts with cheerfulness and prosperity than to question one's own philosophy and faulty actions.

As you live a fulfilling life, some people will dislike you, simply because you are a reminder of what IS possible for a human being.

You can't please everyone. When you're too focused on living up to other people's standards, you aren't spending enough time raising your own. Some people may whisper, complain and judge. But for the most part, it's all in your head. People care less about your actions than you think. Why? They have their own problems! – Kris Carr

I have made the choices that work best for me. I know I cannot please everyone, and that's fine. – Marlee Matlin

When you stand alone and sell yourself, you can't please everyone. But when you're different, you can last. – Don Rickles

The Rich make sure to lose little time to feeling upset that others are displeased. The Rich focus on the next action to further their goals.

Principle: Be the best version of yourself. Avoid being a "people pleaser."

Have you compromised yourself or your work to please everyone? How can you better support how you are different and provide unique benefits to those who want to be connected to you and your work?

Drop Time-Wasters #2

Drop Hesitation that Arises When You Can't See Every Future Step

Just tonight, as I led a workshop *Discover Your Enchanted Prosperity*, an audience member asked me, "How can you prevent a new business from failing?"

I shared a process I call "I.A.M."

1. **Identify** what is the final transaction that brings in money.

2. **Arrange** that the project remains attractive for subsequent rounds of funding.

3. **Measure** carefully and control the "burn rate."

(The *burn rate* is how much money is used each month to simply keep the business functioning.)

We cannot anticipate all that might happen. You may have an excellent product but the marketplace is *not* interested at the moment. For example, the feature film *The Princess Bride* failed at the box office. However, it has done millions of dollars of business on VHS, DVD and Blu-ray. The enduring quality of *The Princess Bride* is well-received as each generation introduces the film to the next generation.

For those people who follow a spiritual path, it helps to include this in your prayers: "This or something better." You acknowledge that you cannot see, at this moment, the ultimate benefits that may arise.

Take the first step in faith. You don't have to see the whole staircase, just take the first step. – Martin Luther King, Jr.

Principle: Take your first step knowing that it creates "this or something better."

What can be your new "first steps"?

_____

_____

_____

Drop Time-Wasters #3

Drop Perfectionism in Favor of Excellence

But I am learning that perfection isn't what matters. In fact, it's the very thing that can destroy you if you let it. – Emily Giffin

Stuck! It was such a different experience. I wrote three blog posts in a row and none of them felt "good enough" to publish. Perhaps, I was rusty. I had stepped away from writing blog posts for a time because I had been traveling and finishing my final draft of a book. Now, I was feeling uneasy about publishing a new blog post. "This is not good enough" was a thought that had me feeling some form of fear.

Understanding the difference between healthy striving and perfectionism is critical to laying down the shield and picking up your life. Research shows that perfectionism hampers success. In fact, it's often the path to depression, anxiety, addiction, and life paralysis. – Brené Brown

At its root, perfectionism isn't really about a deep love of being meticulous. It's about fear. Fear of making a mistake. Fear of disappointing others. Fear of failure. Fear of success.
– Michael Law

Fear is something I know well. Every time, I've done something big, and for the first time, fear shows up. That means it shows up every year for me. I'm doing new things every year. I don't wait for fear to be silent. I just want to quiet down fear a bit, and I'll step forward.

Perfectionism has never heard that anything worth doing is worth doing badly—and that if we allow ourselves to do something badly we might in time become quite good at it. Perfectionism measures our beginner's work against the finished work of masters. Perfectionism thrives on comparison and competition.
– Julia Cameron

The Solution for Perfectionism and Related Fear: *Set Criteria for Excellence*

In another section of this book, I mention **Set Criteria for Excellence.** It's an essential process. Ask yourself:
- What must be in this project?
- What do the end users absolutely need in this project?
- What can I learn along the way in doing this project?
- What can I drop from this project to make it more manageable?
- How can I recover if the results do not turn out in my favor?

The idea with Set Criteria for Excellence is that you make good choices. You're not aiming for perfection. You're aiming for excellence and your personal growth during the process.

Having a plan to recover if the project fails to yield good results ***helps you quiet down fear.***

I've had projects fail. Some books have not sold enough copies. On some occasions, I've re-imagined such books and renamed them. We don't know what will happen until we place a product into the marketplace.

Back to my fear of publishing a blog post, I set criteria for excellence. I asked myself these questions: a) Am I telling the truth? and b) Can this blog post help someone? I said yes and posted a blog article!

Step forward.

Principle: Set Criteria for Excellence and quiet down fear. Take action.

What would you place in your Criteria for Excellence?

_____

_____

_____

_____

Drop Time-Wasters #4

Drop Your Preconceptions and Listen

"That's good art, Tom. But it won't sell books," my associate art director said to me when we were in the middle of designing the cover of my book, *The Hidden Power of the AND-Universe.* My concern was that we were going to fall back on the old stand by of a cold photo of stars. I was proposing an odd variant on mountains, a lake and some unusual detail.

With "it won't sell books," my associate art director had picked great words to get me to *drop* my first design ideas and perception of what might make a good image.

The Rich know that getting great advice and listening to that great advice will help them increase their income.

One of my favorite stories comes from fellow author-speaker Allen Klein. He tells of the time when he was in the kitchen and could not find a serving spoon he put down moments before. He looked around and couldn't see the spoon. Finally, he took a step to the side—Then he could see the spoon that had been obscured by a napkin! **A simple step to the side changed his view and perception.**

We're invited to "side step" at various moments in life.

 Your perspective on life comes from the cage you were held captive in. – Shannon L. Alder

You and I possess a great gift: We have the freedom to take efforts to observe what "cage" we may have been living in. What are the bars of such a cage? Limiting beliefs.

Gratitude can open your thoughts.

Be thankful for what you have; you'll end up having more. If you concentrate on what you don't have, you will never, ever have enough. – Oprah Winfrey

We are all in the gutter, but some of us are looking at the stars. – Oscar Wilde

Change the way you look at things and the things you look at change. – Wayne W. Dyer

Principle: Make a shift so you can see your life from a new, empowering perspective.

What are your habitual thoughts? Are they limiting you? What empowering thoughts could you focus on to shift your perception?

_____

_____

_____

_____

Drop Time-Wasters #5

Drop Trying to Hold onto Every Friend

Some friends are like belts; you eventually outgrow them.
– Larry Winget

Life has many chapters, and a new chapter can start at any minute.

When a friend gives you signs that they want to leave, it's often wise to *listen*. The signs may show that it's time for you to enter a *new chapter* of life *without* that particular friend.

It's strange that a number of individuals I've observed seem to need to make a scene in order to justify to themselves that they can end a situation.

One time I saw a particular friend "Gertrude" abandon one of my clients. Gertrude had to make my client wrong and then Gertrude could justify why she left my client in a tough position.

Some people hold onto their precious, caustic beliefs like a security blanket. As you grow beyond such beliefs, these people will WASTE YOUR TIME providing *needless drama*.

The Rich do NOT allow people to waste their time. The Rich are too busy making what they want to manifest.

I used to think that as a loyal friend I needed to endure a lot of bumpy times and do a LOT of listening. Then I learned—the hard way—to truly listen and observe the signs of someone who wanted (or needed) to drift out of my life.

At this moment, as I write this, I think of two people who are not in this chapter of my life. I get sad for a moment. Then I think: "Thank you. You were good part of a previous chapter of my life." I then say a prayer for the two people to be happy and whole in their own lives.

In a number of cases, I have realized that it was time to release both myself and that friend-of-a-previous-chapter.

I have a phrase: *I release me. I release you. I'm not the same. You're not the same. It's a new chapter. Be well—may you move on in peace and love.*

"Surround yourself with only people who are going to lift you higher," said Oprah Winfrey (as I noted before).

It's true that sometimes a good friend will go through a rough patch. So it may prove beneficial to stand by them.

On the other hand, a "frenemy" is someone who seems like a friend but acts like an enemy and undermines your happiness and wholeness. Be truthful with yourself. End your interactions with this person. Sure, you will grieve, but it's better than having your precious energy drained away. I wrote this:

Some friendships are novels.
Some friendships are short stories.
Some friendships are a sentence.
Put a period on that and get away!

How do you know if a friend is no longer a real friend?

Ask yourself these questions:
- Does this strengthen me?
- Does my success make this person TOO uncomfortable and do they undermine my happiness and wholeness?
- Is this relationship healthy or is it sick?
- Is this person living in an unhealthy way so to protect my own well-being I need to get away?

Principle: Be careful of your friendships. Let go of those who do not support your happiness and wholeness.

Who is someone who cuts you down? Let them go.

Drop Time-Wasters #6

Drop Fear-based "Cover All the Bases"

You cannot swim for new horizons until you have courage to lose sight of the shore. – William Faulkner

A ship is safe in harbor, but that's not what ships are for. – William G.T. Shedd

Happiness is a risk. If you're not a little scared, then you're not doing it right. – Sarah Addison Allen

We must have courage to bet on our ideas, to take the calculated risk, and to act. Everyday living requires courage if life is to be effective and bring happiness. – Maxwell Maltz

In one of my *Discover Your Enchanted Prosperity* workshops, I asked, "What is an obstacle between where you are now and where you REALLY want to be?
An audience member said, "Shadows of past failures."
In an extended discussion, I shared these ideas:
"To quiet down fear so you move forward, it really helps to change your story about a so-called past failure.
I helped one client identify 3 Goals she had for a project. She learned that she had accomplished two of the three goals. True—the project did not make money, but she moved her career forward and the project served more than a thousand people."

An audience member said, "Oh, find the silver lining."

"I replied, "It's even better than that. **When you change the story you tell yourself, you change your neural pathways of your brain.** We're not talking about putting a 'happy face' on a bad situation. We're talking about you experiencing the wisdom and empowerment you gained from stepping into the world and doing something. You're wiser and stronger now. That's real power."

A [person] should never be ashamed to own he has been in the wrong, which is but saying... that he is wiser today than he was yesterday. – Alexander Pope

You don't learn to walk by following rules. You learn by doing, and by falling over. – Richard Branson

Principle: Change the story you tell yourself and create empowering neural pathways in your own brain.

Pick one of your "complaining stories." Now write it here in a *new version* full of learning and how you're wiser and stronger now:

_____

_____

_____

Drop Time-Wasters #7

Drop a Bad Mood; Replace it with a "Tai Chi Calm Down Move" or a "Tai Chi Rev Up Move"

In my *Discover Your Enchanted Prosperity* workshops, I lead the audience through two different Tai Chi movements. Some of us feel frantic at some point in our day. This interferes with our decision-making. The Rich know that making good decisions helps them increase their income. It truly helps to have a process to calm down:

Tai Chi Calm Down Move

Start in a standing position with your feet placed directly below your shoulders. Place your hands at your sides, in a relaxed manner. Bring your hands up until they're straight out (forward). Pull your hands back toward your shoulders, then bring them down to rest at your sides. *(See the image on the next page).* Practice belly-breathing as you do this movement process. Breathe in as your raise your hands. Hold your breath for a moment. Breathe out as you bring your hands down.

Tai Chi Rev Up Move

Some of us get sleepy or simply need more energy before a High Impact Moment (like a vital meeting). The Rich know that one needs to look full of energy and fully confident. It truly helps to have a process to rev up:

Start in a standing position with your feet placed directly below your shoulders. Place your hands in a praying position in front of your chest. Raise your hands skyward. Stretch upward. Have your hands each trace a separate circle (going in opposite directions. Then bring your hands together in the praying position. Keep your knees loose and rise upward with your legs as you go to full extension at the apex of your movement. *(See the image below)*. Practice belly-breathing as you do this movement process. Breathe in as your raise your hands. Breath out as you bring your hands down.

Tai Chi Calm Down Move

Side View | Pull Hands Toward Shoulders | Hands Down

Tai Chi Rev Up Move

Principle: Use Tai Chi movements to improve your mood.

How will you change your mood? Will you use the two Tai Chi moves? Will you employ some other ways to use your body to improve how you're feeling?

Drop Time-Wasters #8

Drop the Path of Burnout

When I speak on the topic *Time Management Secrets for More Productivity PLUS Wellness,* I share how to avoid burnout. Burnout is a huge loss of momentum and time. It truly hurts and demoralizes a person.

To share ways to avoid burnout, I speak of the W.E.L.L. process:

W – walk around burnout-habits
E – energize with "Green Tranquility Goals"
L – linger on the positive
L – lift your mood through structure

1. Walk around burnout-habits

One of my friends, as a 13-year-old girl, felt horrible when she walked past an elementary school, and bullies would shout horrible things simply because she had red hair.

She learned *to walk another way home.* She walked around and away from those tormentors.

Similarly, we need to walk away from "burnout habits." Burnout habits are those that create lack of sleep, excess weight, and constant, harmful stress.

One way to gain strength is to declare certain times of one's day as "technology free." No cells phones during dinner with your loved one can give you a needed respite and enhance closeness. Such closeness can empower you and also gets your body chemistry on your side—your body releases the bonding hormone oxytocin.

2. Energize with "Green Tranquility Goals"

One of my favorite questions is: *Does this strengthen me?* To strengthen yourself, you need goals that are in a realm outside "increase shareholder value." You need **"Being Goals"**—goals that enhance your inner peace and mental and physical health. A *Green Tranquility Goal* of walking 20 minutes a day outside can improve your health and feelings of well-being.

3. Linger on the positive

What's a quick road to burnout? A lack of structure and lack of *a daily method to see all that is well in your life in this moment.* With my clients, I emphasize the *Daily Journal of Victories and Blessings.* A victory is something you accomplish. A blessing is something that arrives that brightens your day—like a surprise phone call with a friend. Neuro-scientists point out that the brain naturally focuses on the negative. Have a negative experience and it immediately goes into one's long-term memory. However, it takes at least *10 seconds of focused attention to get a good experience into your long-term memory.* I've learned that writing in my Daily Journal of Victories and Blessings for 2 minutes just before I go to sleep has me going to sleep happy.

4. Lift your mood through structure

Do you know what reliably lifts your mood? I call an activity that raises your spirits *a healthy mood-lifter.* It can be simply painting a picture for 15 minutes in the morning before you go to work. Take out your calendar and schedule in something that lifts your spirits.

An important part of maintaining a positive structure in

your daily life is to **identify "Droppables."** *Burnout arises, in part, when we keep adding to our schedule and fail to DROP nonessentials from our schedule.*

Picture this. You look at your current schedule and you say, "My plate is full." Then it appears necessary that you'll need to *empty part of your plate.* One therapist I know calls it backing down to 80% of your capacity.

Drop one thing from your schedule and you'll start to feel better. One of my clients said, "It gives me hope. Hope that I can relax for some portion of my day!"

Principle: Carefully add actions that support your inner peace and also pick "droppables" to relieve your schedule.

What will you drop from your schedule ("droppables")? What daily self-nurturing activities will you add to your schedule—to support your well-being?

_____

_____

_____

_____

_____

_____

Bonus One:
Enlightenment Can Clear Your Way, Save You Time and Help You Feel Happy

Nonresistance, nonjudgment, and nonattachment are the three aspects of true freedom and enlightened living." – Eckhart Tolle

Three things—resistance, judgment and attachment—can truly waste our time. Such wasted time can be filled with frustration and emotional pain.

Now I'll share some brief comments related to Eckhart Tolle's above comment on true freedom and enlightened living.

1. Nonresistance

What is the difference between persisting and wasting time? Each one of us must develop our own criteria around this question.

Persisting can be helpful—for one's career. For example, I persisted for years to finally express a story *Living*. First, I wrote a screenplay that served to get me into the film industry. The then-California Film Commissioner read my screenplay. He was impressed, and he said that my screenplay stood out by having more heart than other screenplays. Some time later, I was directing a feature film, and the California Motion Picture Commissioner secured for me San Luis Obispo Airport and an American Eagle airplane for a climatic scene. Through his influence, there was no charge! That helped me have major production value for a tiny budget feature film.

Later, I made an audio novel from the *Living* story.

And recently, my favorite version of the *Living* story is in my collection of fiction titled, *Droids to Magic: Fantastic Tales of Science Fiction and Wonder*.

In certain cases, persistence yields great results. My persistence in refining the *Living* story has served as a great practical classroom for me. I've learned much.

However, putting up resistance in other situations can simply be a waste of effort and time.

Consider these questions:
- In this situation, am I hoping in vain for someone else to change in some grand, unlikely manner?
- Am I going to the wrong person for what I need?
- Am I twisting myself and my values in the name of just getting someone's approval?

Be aware of trying to resist how Life opens a new chapter for you.

One year I found that a friendship with "George" came to an end. I found that a new chapter of my life had opened—a chapter without George. Some people try to cope with loss and grief by changing their whole perception of a friendship. They might say: "Oh, she really wasn't my friend."

Why might they say this? They're resisting. They want to remove value from the friendship they lost.

I suggest avoiding this pattern. Instead, I told myself, "George had been a great friend for that chapter of my life. And I had been a good friend to George."

2. Nonjudgment

"You're wrong," Milton, one of my elderly relatives, says often. Inside, I say to myself, "I'm different. I want things you don't want. I'm willing to pay certain prices (in effort and focus) that you never were willing to."

What does holding judgments cost Milton? The loss of

closeness with multiple family members. One family member will not even step into the building where Milton lives. She won't put up with the negative energy that Milton's judgment entails.

We hear from some people: "Judgment is necessary. How else do we learn from the past?"

Let's take a look.

Judgment often includes someone *acting like a judge*—a superior being looking down and making pronouncements.

On the other hand, one can have **discernment,** during which one is flexible and one makes observations. And one is open to taking in new data.

So one can learn from past situations and still be flexible to see if something has changed in the present.

3. Nonattachment

I've worked with clients and supported them to Big Success! Some of them have felt surprised and disappointed. Why? Because the actual experience after achieving something personally meaningful turns out to be different than one's first imaginings. Sometimes better, sometimes worse—in any case, different.

When you learn to hold "preferences" as opposed to "demands," you acquire a new freedom! How?

You avoid remaining in the mood of "disappointed."

You are flexible. You flow like a leaf on a stream of water. This is the power of nonattachment.

Picture an Aikido martial artist who *simply sidesteps out of the way* of an opponent's punch.

The Rich who function as effective entrepreneurs practice all three processes: nonresistance, nonjudgment and nonattachment.

When Steve Jobs returned to Apple, he immediately cancelled many projects. He was nonattached to those projects.

People think focus means saying yes to the thing you've got to focus on. But that's not what it means at all. It means saying no to the hundred other good ideas that there are. You have to pick carefully. I'm actually as proud of the things we haven't done as the things I have done. Innovation is saying no to 1,000 things.
– Steve Jobs

Principle: Develop true flexibility to seize opportunities: Use the approach of nonresistance, nonjudgment and nonattachment.

In what areas would your life improve if you practice nonresistance, nonjudgment and nonattachment? How would this help your ways of increasing income?

_____

_____

_____

_____

_____

Bonus Two:
Time Management Secrets for More Productivity PLUS Wellness

A significant number of rich people get a lot done because they take good care of their bodies. In this way, they can work more efficiently because their brains function better. They have less "fuzzy moments."

When I speak on the topic "Time Management Secrets for More Productivity PLUS Wellness," I mention this process L.I.V.E. — as in "live better."

L – link you current behavior to Improved Behavior
I – increase sleep
V – "victory-focus"
E – energize

1. Link you current behavior to Improved Behavior

A number of people basically drop a new behavior in their life as if they dumped a grand piano into their bathroom. It just doesn't work.

For example, I have a client who knows that he can get some *light* weight training in, if he does his bicep curls while watching TV. He's not, at this time, signing up for the gym and using 30 minutes to travel to the gym, 60 minutes at the gym and 30 minutes for returning home.

He tells me that two hours is too big a burden at this time.

A number of people long for a breakthrough. It's understandable. Still, for long-term improvement, I discuss what I call an *Easethrough*. **You take obstacles OUT of your way.**

Observe how you can add something to your life in a nondisruptive manner. Take small actions—as your beginning.

2. Increase sleep

The first step to increase your sleep is to log it. Then find ways to change your schedule. Some people find it helpful to set an alarm to ring one hour before their bedtime. Then they do a set of rituals to cool down. They avoid TV during that hour. They have avoided food and exercise for two hours (or three) before bedtime. Sleep is so vital that it helps to study about how to improve your experience and duration of sleep.

3. "Victory-focus"

I'm coining a word here "victory-focus"—as in focus on a victory everyday. Why? The truth is too many people get caught up in a faulty cycle of "punishing themselves too much."

Instead, we use a *Daily Journal of Victories and Blessing*. What is a victory? Anything you accomplish that helps you feel good. Walking 20 minutes at lunch time comprises a victory. Another form of victory is holding your calm while a family member says something that unsettles you.

A blessing is a gift from the universe like a surprise, enjoyable phone call from a friend.

Write in your *Daily Journal of Victories and Blessings* for 2 minutes before you go to sleep at night. You'll go to sleep happy.

4. Energize

Nurture yourself and you increase BOTH your wellness and your productivity. What really works is to rotate challenge, activity and recovery.

If you experience no challenge in your life, you'll likely

feel bored and a lack of energy. People were designed to enjoy games.

For years I've talked about the attraction of video games: a) you get instant feedback, b) you can get better at playing the game, and c) you can win (in incremental ways).

Make sure you have some form of challenge and ways to win. I say, "Make it a game you can win." For example, I note that at this moment, I've written 29,186 words of this book. I'm making progress, and that feels great!

Be sure to plan and take action for your Recovery. This might be a hot, relaxing bath while reading a fun novel. This might be a simple 10 minute walk near trees. It's vital to schedule some Recovery each day. Please note that Recovery is not "numbing out." Some people say that TV-watching is their recovery. That may be a poor substitute for Recovery. *Recovery refreshes you.* It is not something to just dull your pain.

I attend speeches on the topic of wellness. I participate with other people doing something that is uplifting (we do enjoy laughing!) and healthy.

Find something that creates Recovery in you.

Principle: Keep the structure of challenge, activity and recovery in your life for maximum wellness and productivity.

How can you bring healthy challenge, activity and recovery into your life?

Bonus Three:
Guidance from Prosperous People

Rich people get a lot done because they know how to delegate and get people to follow their lead. Here are insights from Mark Sanborn.

8 Reasons Why People Won't Follow You

by Mark Sanborn, CSP, CPAE

There's a familiar saying that if nobody is following you, you're just out taking a stroll. The question for leaders "out taking a stroll" is why nobody is following them?

If you're a leader and people aren't following you, consider the possible reasons:

1. They don't like you.
Research shows we'd rather work with incompetent people who are nice than competent people who aren't. If you treat people poorly and are generally unlikable, it is unlikely anybody will follow you unless they are scared to death to do otherwise. The notable exception in business history have been those unlikable leaders who had such visionary products that others were willing to put up with their behavior. The question remains, however: how much more successful had these high fliers been if they'd paid more attention to likability?

2. They don't trust you.
I have a friend who is a blast to drink beer with. He's always got funny stories and the latest dirt to share. He

discloses lots of things about others. And while I "like" him, I don't trust him. I know that when he's drinking beer with someone else, I'm likely to be the topic of his talking out of school.

I think trust is even more important than likability. While I may not like someone in a business situation, I can still do business with them without fear of being unjustly harmed or cheated.

3. They don't want to go where you're leading.

People are unwilling to go anywhere that doesn't represent a positive change. They can even handle the challenges and sacrifices of a new undertaking if they believe there is a payoff on arrival.

One client had a vision statement that was heavy on financial metrics but said nothing about the quality of life for employees or customers. I wasn't surprised that nobody could remember what the vision was, nor care about achieving it. Their vision statement became effective when it was rewritten to express the future for all stakeholders, including employees.

4. They don't know why they should do what you ask.

Kim is a young leader who is very focused and task-oriented. She is well known for issuing edicts and delegating tasks without explanation. She believes it makes her more time effective, and if anyone asks why, she calmly replied, "Because I said so."

"Because I said so" is tough for kids to swallow and more difficult for adults. Knowing why a request is made is something any intelligent adult would desire. Harried, leaders, however are often better at giving commands than explaining them or providing context.

5. They don't think you have their best interests at heart.

There are times you may ask an employee to do something simply because it is a condition of their job. Don't, however, think that subterfuge, spin or trickery is fair play. It will undermine your credibility. Be honest in the direct payoff—or lack thereof.

If you accomplish organizational goals at the expense of your team members, your legacy is that of tyrant. As overused as the phrase win/win may be, it is still a guiding principle of leaders who get followed.

6. The don't feel supported and/or appreciated.

Just because you pay people to work with you doesn't mean they don't deserve appreciation. A sincere thank you goes a long way towards a motivated team. And support means you care enough to remove barriers and provide the resources your team needs to win.

7. They don't have the training necessary to be good followers.

Phil is a beloved leader. When he picks someone to lead an important project, his initial conversation always includes this question: "Is there anything you'll need to learn now to be successful?"

No amount of motivation will help an employee succeed if he or she doesn't posses the necessary skills. It you are leading a technology initiative, begin by identifying the skills it will take for employees to support you in the change.

8. They don't respect you.

People respect you for who you are, your competence and abilities, and your relationships with others. Who a follower chooses to follow and why tells much about him or her.

That's why people are reluctant to follow others lacking integrity, ability or people skills. By giving allegiance to someone you don't respect, you loose a little self-respect in the process.

Nobody is perfect all the time, but those who get followed devote more time and effort to being the kind of leader who deserves to get followed.

Mark Sanborn is the president of Sanborn & Associates, Inc., an idea lab for leadership development. Leadershipgurus.net lists him as one of the top 30 leadership experts in the world. He has presented speeches and seminars in every state and 12 foreign countries. Mark is the author of eight books, including the bestseller *The Fred Factor: How Passion In Your Work and Life Can Turn the Ordinary Into the Extraordinary* which has sold more than 1.6 million copies internationally. His other books include *You Don't Need a Title to be a Leader: How Anyone, Anywhere Can Make a Positive Difference* and his latest book, *Fred 2.0: New Ideas on How to Keep Delivering Extraordinary Results Do.* Mark is a past president of the National Speakers Association and winner of The Cavett. Mark was awarded The Ambassador of Free Enterprise Award by Sales & Marketing Executives International. www.marksanborn.com

* * * * * *

The Rich know that consistently maximizing efficiency creates the results that increase income. Now Laura Stack shares important methods:

Running a Tight Ship: 4 Ways to Maximize Efficiency
by Laura Stack, MBA, CSP, CPAE

Maximizing personal and team productivity requires notable efficiency. Make sure these practices get your attention:

1. Leverage Technology. Embrace and encourage new trends, devices, and software as they appear. Let your workers use their own devices for business purposes if they want. Why not take advantage of a productivity source you don't have to pay for? Meanwhile, provide instant "anywhere" access to workplace information. Let team members work from alternate locations with Wi-Fi when it's practical. When a member of my office manager's family is ill, it's easy to let her work from home for the day, so she can still be productive. With Wi-Fi, Evernote, and all the snazzy apps we have access to, workers can tap into work information no matter where they are. Give them a secure, reliable way to share ideas and communicate, allowing more flexibility and change-responsiveness.

2. Set and Track Efficiency Goals. Once you've pared your ideas down to size and established goals with your team, set specific schedules for achievement. As with any project, break goals into manageable pieces, each with its own milestones and deadlines. Once you've achieved a goal, retune and set a new one.

3. Measure Everything. You can better influence things when you can understand them, so keep an eye on all the metrics that matter for your team. Use an accountability system, project management software, SharePoint, a common spreadsheet on Google Docs, Outlook Task Assignments, or a scoreboarding system that tracks important team metrics. The systems you use can be off-the-shelf or proprietary; it doesn't matter as long as you use them consistently.

4. **Brainstorm Regularly.** Meet with your team periodically to exchange ideas on how best to achieve your strategic priorities and improve processes and procedures. Look for areas of overlap and eliminate redundancy. Discuss what your team is doing that lacks value. Remove steps that no longer apply when something changes, and make sure each person documents everything, so new people can get up to speed quickly. Remove your thought-filters and let your ideas cross-fertilize to see what kinds of interesting hybrids result. Consider concepts from other fields, and how they might apply to yours. What would you love to do if it were possible?

The Benefits of Consistent Training

For your team members to be productively efficient *and* effective, they need the right tools. This is an indispensable ROI tactic. Some personnel need blazing-fast computing power; others need smartphones and tablets that let them work on the go; still others might require specialized instruments to maximize their performance. Whatever the case, *all* of them need consistent training, undertaken as often as necessary to stay ahead of the changes rolling through your field.

No one wants to spend money if they don't have to. But remember: in business, what matters isn't what you spend *now*, but how much money you make *later*. You have to make short-term investments for long-term gain. It's all about ROI. Done correctly, training produces the extraordinary levels of ROI you need to stay ahead of the game.

Laura Stack, MBA, CSP, CPAE, aka The Productivity Pro®, gives speeches and seminars on sales and leadership productivity. For over 25 years, she's worked with Fortune 1000 clients to reduce inefficiencies, execute more quickly, improve output, and increase profitability. Laura is the author of seven books, including *Doing the Right Things Right: How the Effective Executive Spends Time*.

* * * * * *

One of the worst wastes of time is to be heading in the wrong direction, and a bad business model can drive your prosperity into the ground. No more! Here is guidance from Jeanna Gabellini.

Turn Your Business Model Upside Down
by Jeanna Gabellini

I never thought much about my business model until almost twenty years into being an entrepreneur. I know: crazy, huh? My model was to get an idea, implement it, and keep doing it… if it was fun. But I didn't have criteria to gauge what was working and what wasn't.

Who cares if I'm constantly reinventing the wheel, as long as I could put food on the table?

Are you doing something similar? Maybe you have a well-thought-out model, **but you're unhappy and not**

producing as much profit as you'd like. Your model might feel confining or boring.

Does your model support freedom and fun?

How about chucking your current model for something better? And what if you created a model that worked in harmony with your behavioral style, values and lifestyle?

What if you kicked it up another notch and created a business model so cool that it put your creativity at an all-time high?

Turn your business model upside down, shake it out and put it together in a way that 100% turns you on. You might be cringing right now at the thought of figuring out a business model. It might sound complicated.

Nah! It can be a simple, easy and creative process. In fact, the end product can fit on an 8.5 x 11 piece of paper.

For this exercise, get your fantasy hat on and ditch the voices of every business expert you've ever heard. Answer the following, not worrying about how each question relates to the next. You're connecting with your Inner Business Expert to speak your heartfelt truth.

- What do you **love doing or offering**? (You're so energized by it that you could do/offer it all day long and be ready for more.)
- **How involved** do you want to be in the process?
- Do you want to **sell to a few or to many**? (You're not worrying about monetizing yet, so be honest about your preference.)
- Who do you **freakin' love** serving?
- Do you enjoy offering **a few things or many**?
- If your business were a **party**, what would be the **theme**? Is it intimate and mellow? Is it high energy with fun food, drinks, and dancing? Are you playing poker and giving awesome prizes? Are people

showing up in costumes, tuxes or jeans?

Get all the components on paper. And if you weren't worried about how all the pieces fit together, what would you be thrilled to offer and in what way? If you weren't worried about offering products and services in the low, mid and high price points what would you offer?

Next, weed out any ideas that seem fun, but won't sustain your passion.

The last step to creating your model is to piece the components together in a way that flows for you and your ideal customers. And your pricing needs to feel good in your heart, yet support the profits you claim as your desired outcome (you might need some coaching on that, right?).

Your business model needs to support you emotionally and financially. There are many models out there; there is no rule that they have to be based solely on what business strategists say.

What can you do now to create a model you LOVE?

Jeanna Gabellini is a Master Business Coach who assists conscious entrepreneurs to double (and even triple) their profits by leveraging attraction principles, proven strategies and fun. Grab her FREE audio on dialing in your biz at http://masterpeacecoaching.com/freecd

* * * * * *

The Rich who are entrepreneurs note that they must study marketing to do well in the marketplace. Now C.J. Hayden shares her insights.

Marketing with the 80/20 Rule
by C.J. Hayden, MCC, CPCC

You know about the 80/20 rule, right? It's the guideline that 80% of your return comes from 20% of your investment. For example, 80% of your referrals come from 20% of the people in your network. 80% of your new business comes from 20% of your prospects. 80% of your new contacts come from 20% of the networking activities you engage in. And so on.

Like all such guidelines, this one is inexact, but helpful. If used correctly, it makes you stop and think. Where are most of your returns coming from? And where is most of your effort going? Imagine how much less time and money you could spend on marketing if you could simply identify the 20% of your current efforts that are really the only ones that matter. You could let go of 80% of what you're doing.

I can't guarantee everyone can do this. Some of you are already pretty smart about how you market yourselves. But here are some places to look:

1. Where are your clients actually coming from? You may think you know the answer to this question, but I find in many cases that people's assumptions don't match the data. Review every client you've worked with in the past two years and try to determine how that client entered your life. Make a list of not just the source of each client, but what you may have done (or made available) to produce clients from that source.

For example, "Referred by Mary Smith. Met her for coffee last month," or "Inquiry from my website. Signed up for my special report two weeks ago." If you can't uncover data like this about every new client, now is the time to start tracking it for the future.

Notice any patterns this analysis suggests, and strategize how you might reproduce these successes. Where could you find more referral sources like Mary Smith? Or what potential referral sources already in your network have you yet to meet for coffee? If most of the new clients originating from your website are those that requested your special report, is that request form available on every page?

2. Where are your highest paying or lowest hassle clients coming from? The quality of your clients can make as much difference to the success of your business as the quantity of them. Select the top 20% of your clients from the list you made above—either the ones that paid you the most or troubled you the least—and consider how you might acquire more clients like them.

Notice not just the source of these top clients, but also what characteristics they might share. You might discover that your highest paying clients are those who themselves are in a higher income bracket. Or that the clients who give you the least trouble are the ones who have worked with professionals in your line of business before. These are valuable clues to where the majority of your marketing efforts should go.

3. What marketing approaches are costing you more money than they bring in? When you can see exactly where your clients are coming from, you can also determine where you're paying too much to get them. Common places for overspending are online and print directory listings, pay-per-click ads, search engine optimization fees, and multiple association memberships.

Compare not just what you are spending on each

potential source of clients to what revenue you received from it, but what profit you ultimately made. A $500 ad that brought you a $500 client has earned you nothing. And an ad that produces many inquiries but little paying business consumes time you could better use to produce income.

4. What are you currently doing that you haven't gotten a single client from? Some marketing techniques take time to pay off, but if you've been using a particular approach for several months and no clients have yet resulted, it's time to reconsider. You probably need to either abandon this approach or fine-tune it.

If you belong to a networking group that isn't producing referrals for you, consider whether you should seek a different group that's a better match for your target market, or stick with the group and start meeting its members for coffee. If you've been cold calling corporate prospects without results, you may need to drop cold calling and focus on referrals and introductions.

By making judicious use of the 80/20 rule, you can eliminate the least productive marketing activities you engage in and ramp up those that are more effective. You can also focus most of your marketing on the client sources and type of prospects that have worked well for you in the past. And that can put you in the 20% of entrepreneurs who have a successful business instead of in the 80% who don't.

C.J. Hayden, MCC, CPCC, is the bestselling author of *Get Clients Now!, Get Hired Now!, The One-Person Marketing Plan Workbook, 50 Ways Coaches Can Change the World*, and over 400 articles. C.J. is a business coach, trainer, and speaker who helps entrepreneurs get clients, get strategic, and get things done. Her company, Wings for Business, specializes in serving self-employed professionals, solopreneurs, and service business owners. www.GetClientsNow.com

* * * * * *

The Rich who accomplish much are careful to squeeze each situation like an orange and get the most juice from it. Communicating to a group requires a lot of thought, planning and rehearsal. Patricia Fripp now shares vital insights:

10 Ways to Make Your Leadership Presentations Powerful
by Patricia Fripp, CSP, CPAE

Executive speech coaching secrets from Patricia Fripp. Do you know the tiny differences that make an enormous impact?

Based on my thirty plus years speaking professionally and coaching executives and leaders I promise you many leaders are foolish enough to believe that because they are experts in their subject matter, they can get their point across effectively with little or no preparation. Wrong!

Many of my executive coaching clients are good and are consistently searching for ways to become great. My goal is to challenge them to have more impact by being powerfully pithy. We do this by reading the transcription of their last important presentation.

Print out your script, and read what came out of your mouth. You will be surprised, shocked, and, like some of my clients, horrified!

To make vast improvements, analyze what you have said, and put your words under a magnifying glass. Look for ways to be clearer, sharper, and more specific. This is much easier when you look at the script rather than listening to the live recording.

As you highlight your script with different color markers, you are looking for the following:

Verbal Tics

"So," "I mean," "Right," "You know what I mean," "To tell the truth."

Highlight or underline these words in yellow.

Lack of Specificity

Specificity builds credibility and clarity. Watch your use of "bunches," "tons," "things," and "stuff." These non-specific words devalue your message, and, therefore, your fee.

Highlight or underline these words in pink.

Clichés

"Think outside of the box," "The writing on the wall," "That and a quarter will get you a cup of coffee," etc. Replace clichés with original phrasing.

Highlight or underline these words in green.

Empty Words

"Out there," "At the end of the day," "Each and every one of you in this room."

Jerry Seinfeld: "I will invest an hour in taking eight words down to five."

Highlight or underline. By now you understand!

Focused Language.

Highlight your "I"s, and rephrase with you-focused language. For example, "I am going to talk about . . ." becomes "You will learn . . ."

Word Choice

A single, suddenly-popular buzzword reminds me of fingernails screeching on a blackboard. It's "stuff."

At one of my client's meetings to launch a new solution that had been a $40 million dollar investment, their charismatic National Sales Manager was delivering a powerful presentation. He lost my respect when I heard, "Our clients need our stuff."

Specificity builds credibility, and your message is more likely to be remembered and repeated.

When you read your actual spoken words, you can change them on your script for future presentations. For example, change "I hope you are leaving with three **things**" to "My challenge to you as you are about to leave is, What are your three **major commitments**?"

Setup Phrase and Impact Phrase.

This is a concept that comes from the world of comedy. We are familiar with the setup phrase and the punch word or phrase that triggers the laughter. When you step on your punch word, you kill or minimize the laughter. In business communications, I call the punch phrase the impact phrase.

The impact phrase comes at the end of a sentence.

In 98% of presentations, any unit of time is a **setup phrase**. For example: "Today," "In the next 45 minutes," "Next quarter," "In 1954," or "In last year's elections."

For impact and memorability, don't say, "To celebrate your accomplishments in **2014** . . ." Say, "To celebrate your

2014 **accomplishments** . . ."

Rather than, "This will be our focus for **the next two days**," use, "For the next two days, this will be **our focus**."

Correct Order

Although this is not how we normally speak or write, it is a much more effective way to speak. The audience can see and understand your message when you present it as follows:

The Fripp When, Where, Who, What Happened Formula

A newscaster would say, "President Obama gave a speech on health care at Yale University yesterday."

The Fripped version: "Yesterday (**When** – "Okay, this is recent history.") at Yale University (**Where** – "Oh, I have never been there. I bet it has great buildings and beautiful grounds."), President Obama (**Who**... "I know who that is.") gave a speech on health care" (**What Happened** is more important than when or where it happened). What came last is most memorable.

Visual Shorthand

Forget pronouns, adverbs, verbs, etc. Think picture words and connecting words.

Consider the sentence, "I walked into the boss's office." The action, emotion, and visual scene changes if you change walked to any of these: ran, sauntered, staggered, skipped, raced, or meandered.

A lawyer client was working on a speech on modern day slavery. She said, "He promised her many **things**." I told her, "No. He promised her a life of **romance** and **adventure.** Those two words help the audience fill in the whole story. They can now understand why a young woman would leave the safety of her home and go off with this man."

* * * * * *

8 Ways to Add Value to Your Message

by Patricia Fripp, CSP, CPAE

Some presenters are silly enough to think that if they talk longer, they are giving more value or getting their point across more effectively. Actually, audiences of any size, from 5 to 500, are eager for content to be presented as efficiently and as memorably as possible.

Here are **eight ways to make your message memorable:**

1. **Build rapport before you speak.** Schmooze!
2. Make your message sound valuable by **using specific language.**
3. **Remove the fluff and the filler and the nonwords.**
4. Get comfortable with silence; **pause.**
5. **Know who your audience is and what they care about.**
6. **Be clear about how to express your big idea**, and strategize about how to sell it.
7. **Open with impact, and get to the point fast.**
8. Remember that **all learning requires repetition and reinforcement.**

As a speaker, it is your job to order, clarify, and intensify information for your audience.

When your message must be memorable, your presentation powerful, and your sales successful, you are well-served by calling **Patricia Fripp.** For over thirty years she has helped executives and sales teams gain a competitive edge through powerful presentations. Fripp is a Hall of

Fame keynote speaker, executive speech coach, sales presentation skills trainer, an online training expert. www.fripp.com

* * * * * *

The Rich who accomplish extraordinary things *avoid getting stuck* because other people do not see them excelling. Now, James Malinchak shares a vital lesson he learned.

ANYTHING is possible if you BELIEVE IN YOURSELF and if YOU don't listen to people who tell you that you're not good enough!
By James Malinchak

It was my father who taught me one of the most important life lessons I've ever learned, which is: "Anything Is Possible If You Believe in Yourself and If You Don't Listen to People Who Tell You That You're Not Good Enough!"

Aside from his railroad job in the local steel-mill, my Dad had a weekend job. Most people don't know that my Dad was a NCAA Division 1 College Football Referee. You may have even yelled at him for calling a penalty on your favorite college team. He officiated games that included Notre Dame, Miami (FL), Pittsburgh, Syracuse, Florida, Army, Navy, Texas, Penn State, Boston College, Tennessee, BYU, North Carolina, and USC to name a few. In December 1987, he was rated one of the top college football officials in the entire nation and was selected to officiate the Orange Bowl Game for the National Championship.

The game was between the Oklahoma Sooners and the Miami Hurricanes live, on ABC Worldwide Television. What amazes me to this day is that my Dad wasn't from a big city with a fancy job or big-shot connections. He lived in the tiny steel-mill town of Monessen, Pennsylvania and was able to accomplish this, despite having many odds against him. The likelihood of someone reaching this high-level of officiating big-time NCAA Division 1 College Football, especially officiating the National Championship Game, is slim.

I once asked my Dad how he was able to achieve these big dreams, despite the odds being against him due to living in a small steel-mill town, being a railroad worker in the steel-mill and basically not having any real connections outside of our area. I will never forget my dad looking me in the eye and saying, "Son, anything is possible if you believe in yourself and if don't listen to people who tell you that you're not good enough!"

WOW! Again, my Dad may not have had any formal college education but he was one of the wisest people I have ever known.

That was a true transformational moment in my life as Dad's words have always stayed in my heart. When odds are stacked against me or when I'm faced with a tough, impossible task, I always think back to that advice from my Dad and reminisce about what my Dad accomplished.

Just goes to show you that: ANYTHING is possible if you BELIEVE IN YOURSELF and if YOU don't listen to people who tell you that you're not good enough!

Thanks Dad!

James Malinchak is recognized as one of the most requested, in-demand business and motivational keynote speakers and marketing consultants in the world. He was featured on the Hit ABC TV Show, Secret Millionaire and was twice named "College Speaker of the Year" (APCA and

Campus Activities Magazine). James has delivered over 2,000+ presentations for corporations, associations, business groups, colleges, universities and youth organizations worldwide. James can speak for groups ranging from 20-20,000. visit: www.Malinchak.com

As a consultant, James is the behind-the-scenes, go-to marketing advisor for many top speakers, authors, thought leaders, business professionals, celebrities, sports coaches, athletes and entrepreneurs and is recognized as "The World's #1 Big Money Speaker® Trainer and Coach" teaching anyone who wants to get highly-paid as a motivational or business speaker how to correctly package, market and sell their time, knowledge, experience, expertise, message, personal story and how-to advice. visit:

www.BigMoneySpeaker.com and

www.CollegeSpeakingSuccess.com

* * * * * *

I'm grateful for the participation of the above prosperous authors.

To put this in few words, **the Rich have a different way of viewing life.** It's good to listen and see how you might want to apply some of their perceptions toward increasing your Sustainable Wealth.

A FINAL WORD AND SPRINGBOARD TO YOUR DREAMS

Congratulations on your efforts as your worked with the material in this book. To get even more value from this book, take the plans and insights that you created and place them in some form in your calendar or day planner. *Plan and take action.* Return to these pages again and again to reconnect with the material and take your life to higher levels.

The best to you,
Tom

Tom Marcoux
Executive Coach and Spoken Word Strategist

Special Offer Just for Readers of this Book:

Contact Tom Marcoux at tomsupercoach@gmail.com for special discounts on **coaching**, books, workshops and presentations. Just mention your experience with this book.

==> See an Excerpt from Tom Marcoux's book, *Darkest Secrets of Persuasion and Seduction Masters: How to Protect Yourself and Turn the Power to Good* — on the next page.

Excerpt from
Darkest Secrets of Persuasion and Seduction Masters: How to Protect Yourself and Turn the Power to Good
by Tom Marcoux, Executive Coach – Spoken Word Strategist
Copyright Tom Marcoux

. . . Now, I am in my 40's, with gray in my hair, and for 27 years I have been taking action to protect people.

And now is the time for me to protect you with the Countermeasures I reveal in this book.

Every human being needs to be able to break the trance that a Manipulator creates.

You need to make good decisions so you are safe and you keep growing—and you are not cut down and crippled.

This Darkest Secrets material is so intense that I first released it only with the counterbalance of my most energizing and uplifting books, Nothing Can Stop You This Year! and 10 Seconds to Wealth: Master the Moment Using Your Divine Gifts.

An interviewer asked me: "Who can be the Manipulator?"

A co-worker, a boss, a salesperson, someone you're dating, and someone you think is a friend.

Now is the time—this very minute—for me to write this book to protect you.

I must speak the truth.

These Darkest Secrets of "persuasion masters" are …

Wait a minute! Let's say it plainly: These are the Darkest Secrets of masters of manipulation. Throughout this book, I will call these people what they are: Manipulators.

Dictionary.com defines "manipulate" as "To influence or manage shrewdly or deviously.… To tamper with or falsify for personal gain."

In this book, we will look on a manipulator as one who deviously influences someone with no concern about that person's well-being, and who causes harm to that person.

Here is the first Darkest Secret:

Darkest Secret #1:
Manipulators Make You Hurt
and Then Offer the Salve.

Manipulators would invite you to go out in the sun for hours and then sell you the salve to soothe your burns. The problem is that we don't notice that this is what they're doing.

For example, you're considering the purchase of a house. A Manipulator asks the question, "So, where would you put your TV?" This question is designed to put you into a trance.

Dictionary.com defines "trance" as "a half-conscious state, seemingly between sleeping and waking, in which ability to function voluntarily may be suspended." Let's condense this: in a trance you may not be able to function freely.

Here is the second Secret:

Darkest Secret #2:
Manipulators Put You into a Trance.

To protect yourself, you must learn to use Countermeasures to Break the Trance.

All the Countermeasures (actions you can take to break the trance) in this book will make you stronger and more capable of protecting yourself.

Now, we'll view the third Secret:

Darkest Secret #3:
Manipulators Care Nothing for You and Human Decency: They'll lie, cheat, and do whatever they need to do so they win—but their charm masks all this.

Let's return to the example of a Manipulator selling you a house. A Manipulator does not pause for an instant to see if you can truly afford the new house. The Manipulator would neglect to mention that you will not only have your mortgage payment of $900. There will be additional costs: home repairs, property tax, water, electricity, homeowner's insurance, and more. The Manipulator only emphasizes what he or she knows you want to hear: "Look! $900 is better than the $1500 you're paying for rent, which is just going down the toilet. And the $900 is an investment."

Let's go back to **Darkest Secret #1:**
Manipulators make you hurt and then offer the salve.

The Manipulator has you feeling good about the solution (salve) and feeling bad about your current life situation.

How? A Manipulator will make you hurt through questions such as:

- What bothers you about paying $1500 a month for rent?

(The Manipulator will use a derisive tone when he says the word *rent*.)

• What is *not* smart about paying rent on someone else's house instead of investing in your own house?

• How do you feel about your children walking in the neighborhood where you live now?

Do you see how these questions are designed to make you hurt enough so that you'll buy?

An interviewer asked me, "Tom, aren't these good arguments for purchasing a house?"

"What we're looking at is the *intention* of the influencer," I replied. "Let's look at our definition of a manipulator as one who deviously influences someone with no concern about that person's well-being, and who causes harm to that person. If the person truly cannot afford the house, he or she will be harmed by buying it. If the manipulator conceals the truth, the manipulator is doing harm. That's the important difference."

Some friends of mine are ethical and helpful real estate agents who truthfully reveal the whole situation and help the purchaser achieve her own goals.

In this book, we are talking about another type of person; that is, unethical Manipulators.

* * *

In any given moment, we need to remember the tactics Manipulators use. We will focus on the word D.A.R.K. so you can remember details easily and protect yourself from Manipulators.

D — Dangle something for nothing
A — Alert to scarcity
R — Reveal the Desperate Hot Button

K — Keep on pushing buttons

1. Dangle Something for Nothing

What do conmen and conwomen do to seize your attention? They make you think you're getting a "steal."

I recently saw a documentary in which a conman on a street in England showed a toy that looked like it was dancing. This fake product was actually dancing because of a hidden, invisible thread. The conman was dangling something for nothing. The Entranced Buyer thought he was getting something worth $20 for only $5. That was the trick. The Entranced Buyer felt that he was getting $15 extra of value for his $5. What the Buyer really got was something worth nothing. Similarly, I know someone who purchased a copy of a Disney movie from a street vendor in San Francisco. She brought the copy home and it was unwatchable—and the street vendor was never seen again.

An old phrase goes, "A conman cannot con someone who is not looking for something for nothing."

How to Protect Yourself from "Dangle Something for Nothing"

Stop! Get on your cell phone and talk through the "deal" with someone you know who thinks clearly. Go home. Think about it. Do some research on the Internet. Listen to your gut feelings. If the salesman or conman is too insistent, get away from that Manipulator. Get quiet. Have a cup of water. Cool down. Break the Trance!

Break the Trance and Identify the Crucial Detail

Earlier, I mentioned that a Manipulator puts you into a trance. An added problem is that we put ourselves into a trance. For example, as you read this, are you thinking about your right toe? Most likely not (unless you stubbed your toe recently). The point is that we only focus on a tiny percentage of what is going on in our life.

Around fifteen years ago, I caused myself trouble because I put myself into a trance. I discovered that under certain conditions, friendship can make you nearly deaf. Here's how: I was producing a song for a motion picture. A good friend was singing backup in the chorus. Because of our friendship, I wanted him to sound great. I completely missed the Crucial Detail. In this kind of situation, the Crucial Detail is that what truly counts is how the lead singer sounds! I made a song that I could not release. What a waste of time and money! I had put myself into a trance.

In any situation in which the Manipulator is "dangling something for nothing," we often fall into a trance and miss the Crucial Detail. The most important detail is *not* that we're saving money if we order before midnight tonight. What counts is whether the product creates a lasting, crucial benefit in our lives. And is the benefit of the product worth the cost? Some people even program themselves to make mistakes by saying, "I can't pass up a bargain." The bargain is *not* the Crucial Detail.

Secrets to Break the Trance

This is the process of B.R.E.A.K.S. It will help you remember the proven methods to break a trance.
B — Breathe
R — Relax
E — Envision
A — Act on aromas
K — Keep moving

S — Smile

Secret #1: Breathe

Remember Secret #1: Manipulators make you hurt and then offer the salve. The Manipulator wants to put you into a state of being that fills you with a sense of urgency and anxiety. Oh, no! I'm going to miss the sale!

Stop this highly vulnerable state. Take a deep breath. Do it now. Take a deep breath and let your belly "get fat" by filling it with air. As you breathe out, let your belly deflate. Breathe in through your nose and breathe out through your mouth. This is called belly-breathing. Repeat the actions of belly-breathing three times. Good. Now, do you feel different? Remember, when you are relaxed, you are strong.

Secret #2: Relax

You become stronger when you condition yourself to relax in the face of adversity. Researchers note that when an Olympic athlete is confronted with the most stressful moment in her life, she has prepared in advance. She has given herself ways to calm down. Two powerful methods are described in this section about B.R.E.A.K.S. One is breathing, and the other is envisioning.

A special part of relaxing is the effective use of your posture …

End of Excerpt from
Darkest Secrets of Persuasion and Seduction Masters: How to Protect Yourself and Turn the Power to Good

Purchase your copy of this book (paperback or ebook) at Amazon.com or BarnesandNoble.com
See **Free Chapters** of Tom Marcoux's 36 books at http://amzn.to/ZiCTRj

ABOUT THE AUTHOR

You want more and better, right? Imagine fulfilling your Big Dream.

Tom Marcoux can help you—in that he's coached thousands of people: CEOs, small business leaders, graduate students (at Stanford University) speakers, and authors.

Marcoux is known as an effective **Executive Coach** and **Spoken Word Strategist.**

(and Thought Leader—okay, writing 36 books helped with that!)

** *CEOs, Vice-Presidents, Other Executives, Small Business Leaders:*

You know that leading people and speaking at your best can be tough.

Marcoux solves problems while helping you amplify your own Charisma, Confidence and Control of Time.

Interested? Email Marcoux—tomsupercoach@gmail.com

Ask for a *Special Report:*

* 9 Deadly Mistakes to Avoid for Your Next Speech

** *Speakers, Experts—for a great TED Talk, Book, Audio Book, Speeches, YouTube Videos.*

Marcoux solve problems while helping you to make your

Concise, Compelling Message that gets people to trust you and get what you're offering (product, service, *an idea*).

Yes—the *San Francisco Examiner* designated Tom Marcoux as "The Personal Branding Instructor."

Marcoux is an expert on STORY. He won a Special Award at the EMMY AWARDS, and he directed a feature film that went to the CANNES FILM MARKET and earned international distribution.

(Marcoux helps you *be heard and be trusted*—a focus point of his 16th Anniversary edition book, *Connect: High Trust Communication for Your Success in Business and Life*.)

As a CEO, Marcoux leads teams in the United Kingdom, India and the USA. Marcoux guides clients & audiences (IBM, Sun Microsystems, etc.) in leadership, team-building, power time management and branding. See Tom's Popular BLOG: www.TomSuperCoach.com

Specialties: coach to CEOS * Executives * Small Business owners * Leaders * Speakers * Experts * Authors * Academics

One of his *Darkest Secrets* books rose to #1 on Amazon.com Hot New Releases in Business Life (and in Business Communication). A member of the National Speakers Association for over 15 years, he is a professional coach and guest expert on TV, radio, and print.

Marcoux addressed National Association of Broadcasters' Conference six years running. With a degree in psychology, Tom is a guest lecturer at **Stanford University**, DeAnza, & California State University, and teaches business communication, designing careers, public speaking, science fiction cinema/literature and comparative religion at Academy of Art University. He is engaged in book/film projects *Crystal Pegasus* (children's) and *Jack AngelSword* (thriller-fantasy). See Tom's well-received blogs

at www.BeHeardandBeTrusted.com

at www.YourBodySoulandProsperity.com

Consider engaging **Tom Marcoux as your Executive Coach.**

"As Tom's client for many years, I have benefited from his wisdom and strategic approach. Do your career and personal life a big favor and get his books and engage him as **your Executive Coach**." – Dr. JoAnn Dahlkoetter, author of *Your Performing Edge* and Coach to CEOs and Olympic Gold Medalists

"Tom Marcoux coached me to get more done in 10 days than other coaches in 2 years." – Brad Carlson, CEO of MindStrong LLC

As the Spoken Word Strategist, Tom Marcoux can help you with **speech writing** and **coaching for your best performance.**

As Tom says, *Make Your Speech a Pleasant Beach.*

Join Tom's Linkedin.com group: *Executive Public Speaking and Communication Power.*

At Google+: join the community "Create Your Best Life – Charisma & Confidence"

Get a **Free** report: "9 Deadly Mistakes to Avoid for Your Next Speech and 9 Surefire Methods" at

http://tomsupercoach.com/freereport9Mistakes4Speech.html

Tom Marcoux has trained CEOs, small business owners, and graduate students to speak with impact and gain audiences' tremendous approval and cooperation. *Learn how to present and get thunderous applause!*

"Tom, Thanks for your coaching and work with me on revising my speech at a major university. Working with you has been so enlightening for me. Through your gentle prodding and guidance I was able to write a speech that connects with the audience. I wish everyone could experience the transformation I have undergone. You have helped me discover the warm and compelling stories that now make my speech reach hearts and uplift minds. This was truly an empowering experience. I cannot thank you enough for your great assistance." — J.S.

"Tom Marcoux has been an NAB Conference favorite [speaker] for six years. And he is very energetic."

– John Marino, Vice President, National Association of Broadcasters, Washington, D.C.

"Using just one of Tom Marcoux's methods, I got more done in 2 weeks than in 6 months."

– Jaclyn Freitas, M.A.

Tom's Coaching features innovations:
- Dynamic Rehearsal
- Power Rehearsal for Crisis
- The Charisma Advantage that Saves You Time

Become a fan of Tom's graphic novels/feature films:
- Fantasy Thriller: *Jack AngelSword*
  type "JackAngelSword" at Facebook.com
- Science fiction: *TimePulse*
  www.facebook.com/timepulsegraphicnovel
- Children's Fantasy: *Crystal Pegasus*
  www.facebook.com/crystalpegasusandrose

See **Free Chapters** of Tom Marcoux's 36 books at http://amzn.to/ZiCTRj   Amazon.com

Your Notes:

_____

_____

_____

_____

Area for Your Sketches of Your Ideas:

www.ingramcontent.com/pod-product-compliance
Lightning Source LLC
Chambersburg PA
CBHW060538100426
42743CB00009B/1566